Crocheted MYTHICAL CREATURES

15 makes from legends, folklore and fairytales

Jacki Donhou

CONTENTS

WELCOME 4
MATERIALS AND TOOLS 8
STITCHES AND TECHNIQUES 10
FINISHING TOUCHES 21
ABBREVIATIONS 23

MEDUSA THE GORGON

FAUN

CHINESE DRAGON

NESSIE THE LOCH NESS MONSTER

GRIFFIN

MERMAID

WOLPERTINGER

THE KRAKEN 36

CERBERUS 44

DJINN 54

BANSHEE 92

CHERRY BLOSSOM DRYAD 104

UNICORN 114

WATER KELPIE 162

MANTICORE 176

ABOUT THE AUTHOR	190
INDEX	190
ACKNOWLEDGEMENTS	191

WELCOME

Hello once again, friends!

As I have said before, even if we haven't met, our community of makers is such a close-knit bunch that we don't feel like strangers. I am incredibly excited to introduce you to my second published book! This new collection showcases the slightly spooky and intriguing world of mythical, legendary and folkloric creatures.

With this book, I wanted to explore more techniques and different styles of amigurumi by bringing to life the mysterious and fearsome creatures that have captured our imaginations and sparked our curiosity for centuries. Whether seen as glorified symbols, fearless protectors or frightening foes, mythical creatures and monsters have a special place in our hearts, reminding us of the endless possibilities and magic that exist in the world.

Like many of you, I am a compulsive collector of yarn. I have a hard time resisting squishy cotton skeins and colourful hand-dyed hanks from my local shops. Over the years since I started designing, my yarn collection has grown to include cotton, merino wool, chenille, blends, roving, yarn cakes, acrylic and so much more. When beginning a new design, it is exciting to map out which weight or kind of yarn will bring this new pattern to life for me. I thought it was important to design these new patterns in a yarn that would complement each creature the way I envisioned the collection: bold and breathtaking. Bamboo Pop yarn from Universal Yarn Brand is a bamboo and cotton blend with a soft feel and is a thin enough yarn to accentuate all the little details. One of the main perks of this yarn is the large assortment of diverse colours it comes in.

I hope you enjoy making these fascinating mythical creatures. It was extremely fun picking and choosing the designs to create and bring to life.

Happy ami making!

Jacki

Materials, Tools and Techniques

MATERIALS AND TOOLS

These are the materials and tools you will need to complete the projects in this book.

YARN

When first crocheting the mythical creatures in this book, take your time and select the yarn brand and weights that you are comfortable with. The collection I chose for this book is Bamboo Pop from Universal Yarn Brand. It is a light and smooth yarn, soft to the touch yet strong enough to handle a tighter tension when crocheting. This light, DK-weight yarn (short for double knitting) is known as 3 light or 6-ply in some countries, and is a blend of 50% cotton and 50% bamboo. This yarn was my personal preference for these designs, but you should choose the yarn in which you'd like to see your creature made.

If you use a different brand or weight of yarn, remember that different yarns will change the size and look of the final creature. Lighter-weight yarns will create smaller items, while heavier-weight yarns will create larger finished projects than those shown in this book.

CROCHET HOOKS

Crochet hooks come in a range of sizes. Finding the right hook size for your amigurumi project and choice of yarn can be difficult. The larger the hook the larger your stitches will be. When working with amigurumi patterns, choosing a hook size two or three sizes smaller than recommended on the yarn label is ideal; this results in tighter stitches with smaller holes for the stuffing to show through. For instance, the recommended hook size for the Bamboo Pop yarns is 4mm, but this would generally be for making wearable items such as scarves, wraps or hats. The projects in this book required a much tighter stitch, so I went down to a 2mm hook to guarantee that the stuffing would not show through the stitches.

CROCHET THREAD

Crochet thread is a very fine mercerized cotton yarn. It is not a thread used for sewing projects but is intended for delicate crochet and knitting crafts such as lace work. It is mostly available in three thicknesses – size 3, size 10 and size 20 – and in a range of colours. I used size 10 for my projects. This is thinner than a lightweight, 4-ply (fingering) yarn and has the most colour options. It makes fine details such as the outlining around the safety eyes and embroidered noses and cheeks more noticeable, which gives more personality to the faces of the amigurumis.

SAFETY EYES

Safety eyes are hard plastic eyes with washer backs. They can be found in craft supply stores. They are available in solid colours, multi-colours, and even glitter for added sparkle. I have used two sizes of solid black eyes for my patterns: ½in (12mm) and 9/16in (14mm). See page 22 for instructions on how to attach them. Please note that if you are making an amigurumi for a young child, it is advisable to embroider the eyes rather than using safety eyes.

STUFFING

Polyester fibre filling is a synthetic hypoallergenic fibre made for pillows, crafts and toys. When you stuff an amigurumi piece, you want it to be firm enough to hold its shape but not be over-stuffed. Follow the steps clearly, as some projects include specific instructions on how to stuff the pieces.

EMBROIDERY NEEDLES

Embroidery needles are long needles with a large eye used to sew together and attach the amigurumi pieces. With my patterns, I tend to use two needles: a larger needle with a blunt tip to sew the body parts together – approximately 7in (17.5cm) in total length, with an eye 1in (2.5cm) long – and a smaller needle with a sharp tip approximately 1½in (4cm) in total length for the eye details. If you find another size needle that works best for you, use the more comfortable size.

SCISSORS

Using a small pair of embroidery scissors with sharp tips is best. When you need to trim yarn ends after fastening off, smaller scissors lessen the risk of cutting through and damaging the other stitches.

SEWING PINS

Use these stick pins to keep all your amigurumi body parts secured and in place for sewing. Pins with a ball or a heart on the top are easier to use and give you something to hold. They are also easier to see against the crocheted surface. Pins with a flat top are not recommended, because they can get lost in your amigurumi pieces. I like to use a lot of pins, so my pieces stay in the correct place and do not move while I am attaching them.

STITCH MARKERS

Stitch markers are plastic or metal clasps that hook onto your crochet work and are designed to keep track of either the starting or the ending stitch in your rounds. As you crochet from round 1 and on, you can move your stitch marker up to the next round.

POMPOMS

A pompom is a small decorative ball of fur or yarn. These are available in different colours and sizes or can easily be made by wrapping yarn around your hand or buying a pompom maker. A pompom is needed for the Wolpertinger's tail; full instructions for making a pompom are given in that project (see page 161), or you can buy a readymade one.

PIPE CLEANERS

A pipe cleaner is a twisted wire covered in soft bristles, sometimes called a chenille stem or craft stick. This craft tool has multiple uses, coming in a large multipack and a variety of colours. The most common size is 12in (30cm) long. In this book they are used for slightly bending and shaping some of the tails and to place inside the neck or limbs of the dolls to keep them upright and sturdy. The instructions for placing them are given in the individual projects.

STITCHES AND TECHNIQUES

Here we explain the crochet stitches and techniques you will need to be familiar with in order to make the projects in this book. With easy-to-follow instructions and clear illustrations, you'll be making the most fabulous amigurumi creatures and dolls in next to no time. Please note that this book uses UK crochet terms.

HOLDING A HOOK

To hold a crochet hook, use your dominant hand to grip the hook and your less dominant hand for holding the yarn.

Hold the crochet hook at a downward angle, like a knife.

HOLDING YARN

There are many ways to hold the yarn while you crochet. It all depends on which hold is the most comfortable for you to maintain the right amount of tension.

If the yarn tension is too tight as you crochet, inserting the crochet hook in the next set of stitches could be difficult. If the tension is too loose, you will create holes in the rounds through which the stuffing could show. Take the time to find a hold that suits you.

Step 1: A simple way to hold the yarn is to begin by wrapping it around your little finger, then carry it under the next two fingers and over the index finger.

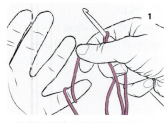

Step 2: Your thumb and middle finger will then grip the tail end of the yarn to hold it in place. Elevate your index finger to add the tension the yarn needs and make your first stitch.

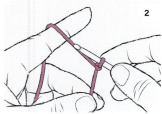

CROCHETED MYTHICAL CREATURES

MAKING A SLIPKNOT

Almost all pieces of crochet will begin with a slipknot.

Holding the yarn end, make a loop by crossing the yarn over itself. Insert the hook through the centre of the loop, yarn over the hook and pull the hook back through the centre. Pull the yarn end to tighten the loop on the hook to create the slipknot.

CHAIN STITCH (ch)

A chain stitch is a basic stitch that is mostly used to start or end a row.

Step 1: Starting with a slipknot, wrap the yarn around the crochet hook.

Step 2: Simply pull the yarn through the loop on the hook to form the first chain.

Step 3: If you need to make several chains, repeat the steps until you have the required number of chains.

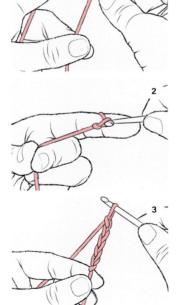

SLIP STITCH (sl st)

The slip stitch has more than one use in a pattern, adding a detailed seam to a piece and sometimes connecting pieces together.

Step 1: Insert the crochet hook under the stitch and wrap the yarn around the crochet hook.

Step 2: Pull the yarn through the stitch and through the loop on the crochet hook. If you need to make several slip stitches, repeat the steps until you have the required number of slip stitches for the pattern.

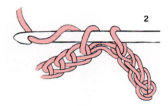

STITCHES AND TECHNIQUES

DOUBLE CROCHET (dc)
Double crochet is the main stitch used for the projects.

Step 1: Insert the crochet hook under both loops of the stitch or the chain space.

Step 2: Wrap the yarn around the crochet hook and pull the yarn through the stitch. There will be two loops on the crochet hook.

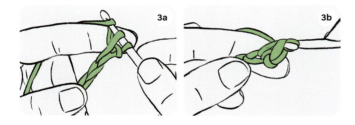

Step 3: Wrap the yarn around the crochet hook once more and pull the yarn through both loops on the crochet hook.

TREBLE (tr)
Treble stitch is a taller version of double crochet.

Step 1: Wrap the yarn around the crochet hook and then insert the hook under the stitch or the chain space.

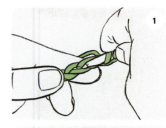

Step 2: Wrap the yarn around the crochet hook and pull the yarn through the stitch. There will be three loops on the crochet hook. Wrap the yarn around the crochet hook again.

Step 3: Pull the yarn through two of the loops on the crochet hook, leaving two loops on the crochet hook. Then, wrap the yarn around the hook once more.

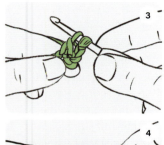

Step 4: Pull the yarn through the last two remaining loops on the crochet hook.

THIRD LOOP
The third loop of a double crochet stitch is on the back side of the row and below the back loop. It runs horizontally like a line or bar behind the stitch. Grab this loop with the point of the hook rather than pushing the hook under the loop; it makes it easier in case the tension is tighter.

DOUBLE TREBLE (dtr)

Double treble stitch is an even taller stitch that starts by wrapping the yarn around the crochet hook twice at the beginning of the stitch.

Step 1: Wrap the yarn around the crochet hook twice, then insert the hook under the stitch or the chain space.

Step 2: Wrap the yarn around the crochet hook and pull the yarn through the stitch. There will be four loops on the crochet hook.

Step 3: Wrap the yarn around the crochet hook again and pull the yarn through two of the four loops on the crochet hook. This will leave three loops on the crochet hook. Wrap the yarn around the crochet hook and pull the yarn through two of the three loops on the crochet hook, leaving two loops on the crochet hook.

Step 4: Wrap the yarn around the crochet hook once more and pull the yarn through the last two loops on the crochet hook to complete the stitch.

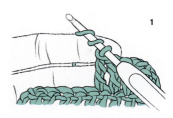

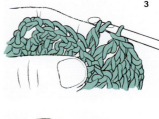

HALF TREBLE (htr)

Half treble stitch is similar to double crochet, but starts by wrapping the yarn around the crochet hook at the beginning of the stitch.

Step 1: Wrap the yarn around the crochet hook, then insert the hook under the stitch or the chain space.

Step 2: Wrap the yarn around the crochet hook and pull the yarn through the stitch. There will be three loops on the crochet hook.

Step 3: Wrap the yarn around the crochet hook once more and pull the yarn through all three loops on the crochet hook.

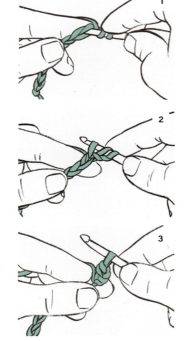

STITCHES AND TECHNIQUES

WORK 2 DOUBLE CROCHET STITCHES INTO THE NEXT STITCH TO INCREASE (dc2inc)

Working two stitches in the same space is a way to make a row or round larger (known as increasing).

Work two of the same stitches in the same stitch or chain space. This will increase the stitch count by one stitch.

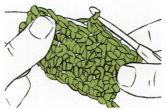

WORK 2 TREBLE STITCHES INTO THE NEXT STITCH TO INCREASE (tr2inc)

Another way to increase a row or a round is to use two treble stitches.

Work two of the same stitches in the same stitch or chain space. This will increase the stitch count by one stitch.

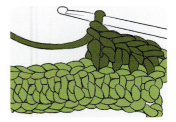

WORK 2 HALF TREBLE STITCHES INTO THE NEXT STITCH TO INCREASE (htr2inc)

Another way to increase a row or a round is to use two half treble stitches.

Work two of the same stitches in the same stitch or chain space. This will increase the stitch count by one stitch.

WORK 2 DOUBLE CROCHET STITCHES TOGETHER TO DECREASE (dc2tog)

A decrease means crocheting two stitches together to shorten a row or round. The method shown here is for an invisible decrease, where the front loops of the two stitches are pulled together so that the back loops collapse behind the stitch to close up the small hole and prevent the stuffing from showing.

Step 1: Insert the hook under the front loop only of the stitch. Then, insert the hook under the front loop only of the next stitch.

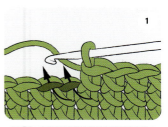

Step 2: With three loops on the hook, yarn over and pull through both the front loops. This leaves two loops left on the hook. Yarn over and pull through the last two loops.

WORK 2 HALF TREBLE STITCHES TOGETHER TO DECREASE (htr2tog)

Another way to decrease a row or a round is to crochet two half treble stitches together, decreasing the stitch count by one stitch.

Step 1: Wrap the yarn around the hook and insert the hook under the first stitch. Then, wrap the yarn around the hook again and draw the yarn up through the stitch. This leaves three loops left on the hook.

Step 2: With three loops on the hook, repeat the first step. Wrap the yarn around the hook and insert the hook under the second stitch. Then, wrap the yarn again and draw the yarn up through that stitch. This leaves five loops left on the hook.

Step 3: Wrap the yarn around the hook for the last time and pull through all five loops.

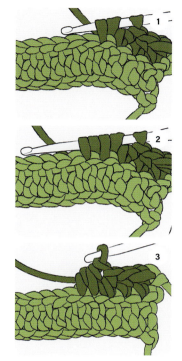

WORK 2 TREBLE STITCHES TOGETHER TO DECREASE (tr2tog)

A third way to decrease a row or a round is to crochet two unfinished treble stitches together. This will decrease the stitch count by one stitch.

Step 1: Wrap the yarn around the crochet hook and then insert the hook under the stitch or the chain space. Wrap the yarn around the crochet hook and pull the yarn through the stitch. There will be three loops on the crochet hook.

Step 2: Wrap the yarn around the crochet hook again. Pull the yarn through two of the loops on the crochet hook, leaving the last two loops on the crochet hook. This makes an unfinished treble crochet.

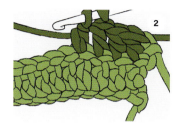

Step 3: Wrap the yarn around the crochet hook and then insert the hook under the second stitch. Wrap the yarn around the hook and pull the yarn through the stitch. There will be four loops on the crochet hook.

Step 4: Wrap the yarn around the crochet hook again, pull the yarn through two of the loops on the crochet hook, leaving the last two loops on the crochet hook. This makes the second unfinished treble crochet and three loops left on the hook.

Step 5: Wrap the yarn around the hook for the last time and pull through the last three loops.

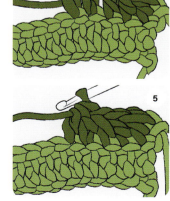

STITCHES AND TECHNIQUES

MAGIC CIRCLE (MC)

The magic circle or ring is the cleanest way to begin a round when crocheting, especially when making amigurumi. It is usually made with double crochet stitches and is an adjustable ring with an end that tightens to close the centre of the first round.

Step 1: Holding the yarn end, make a loop by crossing the yarn over itself. Then, grip that crossing point, insert the hook through the centre of the loop, wrap the yarn around the crochet hook, and pull the hook back through the centre.

Step 2: While still holding the circle, wrap the yarn around the crochet hook and pull the yarn through the loop on the hook to form the first chain. This step is worked around the circle.

Step 3: Insert the crochet hook through the circle, wrap the yarn around the hook and pull the yarn through. There will be two loops on the crochet hook.

Step 4: Wrap the yarn around the crochet hook once more and pull the yarn through both loops on the crochet hook.

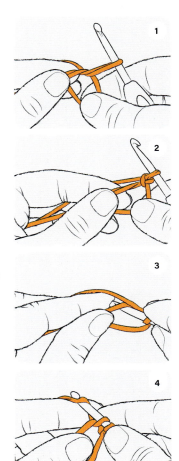

Step 5: This completes the first double crochet stitch on the magic circle. Repeat the steps until you have the number of double crochet stitches for the pattern.

Step 6: Gently pull the yarn end to tighten and close the magic circle. Note that a few pieces like the ears on the dolls will instruct you not to close the magic circle at the end.

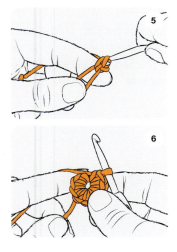

BOBBLE STITCH (BOB)

Bobble stitches are little puffy balls crocheted into the pattern to add toes and thumbs. They are made from six unfinished treble crochet left on the hook within the same stitch and then closed at the end.

Step 1: Yarn over and insert the hook under the next stitch. Yarn over and pull through the stitch, yarn over again and pull through two stitches. Repeat these steps five times until there are six loops on the hook.

Step 2: Yarn over and pull through all six loops.

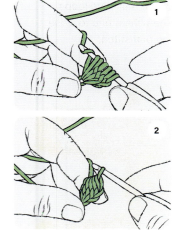

PUFF STITCH (PUFF)

Puff stitches are small, raised stitches which pop up and give a small, detailed texture. They are made from grouping five unfinished, half double crochet stitches in the same stitch and then closed at the top to make them pop out.

Step 1: Yarn over and insert the hook under the next stitch. Yarn over and pull through the stitch. This leaves three loops on the hook.

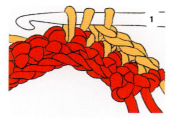

Step 2: Yarn over and insert the hook under the same stitch. Yarn over again and pull through the stitch. Repeat these steps two more times until there are nine loops on the hook.

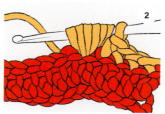

Step 3: Yarn over one last time and carefully pull through all nine loops. Then chain one to close the puff stitch.

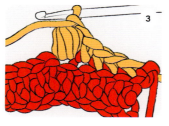

FRONT LOOP ONLY (FLO)

The front loop of the stitch is the loop that is closest to you and the only loop the crochet hook will work under, leaving the BLO unworked. Working FLO stitches changes the positioning of the stitches and curves your next rounds or rows forward. This technique is also used when closing up a piece made from bottom to top by tightening up the last round.

Insert the hook under the loop of the next stitch that is nearest you, not under both loops of the next stitch.

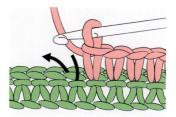

BACK LOOP ONLY (BLO)

The top of a stitch has two loops: a front loop and a back loop. The back loop is the loop that is the furthest from you and the only loop the crochet hook will work under, leaving the closest loop, the front loop, unworked. When working in the back loop only, it changes the effect of the piece you are working on. It reshapes your work and forces the stitches back from their original position.

Insert the hook under the loop of the next stitch that is furthest away, not under both loops of the next stitch.

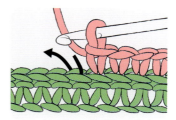

STITCHES AND TECHNIQUES

POPCORN STITCH (POP)

Popcorn stitches are small, oval-shaped puffy stitches crocheted into the pattern to add details. They are made from five treble crochet in the same stitch and then closed at the top to make them stand out.

Step 1: Start by making five treble crochet in the designated stitch.

Step 2: Carefully remove the hook from the last loop, leaving it intact for later, and insert the hook back under the top stitch of the first treble.

Step 3: Grab the last loop with the hook and pull through the stitch.

CHANGING COLOURS

When working on a pattern using multiple colour yarns, colour changes within the specific rounds are necessary.

Step 1: When you need to change a colour in a round, leave the last stitch of the previous colour unfinished without pulling the final loop through the stitch.

Step 2: Wrap the new colour around the hook and pull through the leftover loops.

Step 3: Continue the new colour in the next stitch or stitches. Tie the loose tails in a knot and leave them inside the crocheted piece.

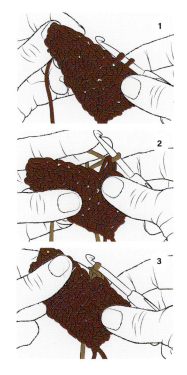

YARN OVER AND YARN UNDER

When discussing how to make your stitches with either yarn over or yarn under, remember there is never a right way or a wrong way; it just comes down to what you are more comfortable with.

Yarn over happens when you hook the yarn strand from underneath, forcing the yarn on top of the hook. When pulled through the stitch to make a double crochet, the result looks like a V-shape.

Yarn under happens when you hook the top of the yarn strand, wrapping it under the hook. When pulled through the stitch to make a double crochet, the result looks like an X-shape.

Working with yarn under, the stitches come out tighter, with fewer holes between them, resulting in a small amigurumi. The yarn over technique has the opposite effect: the stitches will come out slightly larger, which in turn makes the resulting amigurumi pieces big.

INVISIBLE FASTEN OFF IN A ROUND

Fastening off in a round can leave a noticeable bump, whereas an invisible fasten off will make a cleaner finish to the round.

Step 1: Cut the end of the yarn leaving a yarn tail of about 4in (10cm). Pull the loop up and out of the last stitch.

Step 2: With a large embroidery needle, thread the tail through the eye of the needle. Before moving on, count the stitches in the round backwards and mark the first stitch of that round. Insert the needle under both of the top loops of the second stitch that is next to the marked stitch. This will overlap the first stitch, ensuring that we keep the same number of stitches in the round.

Step 3: Pull the needle up and insert it underneath the back loop of the last stitch in the round. This is the same stitch the yarn started from. Weave in the tail on the back or inside of the piece.

FASTEN OFF IN A ROW

Fastening off at the end of a row is very important. Leaving the tail end of the yarn exposed or loose can result in the piece unravelling and you losing all your hard work. Properly fastening off can prevent that from happening.

Cut the end of the yarn leaving a yarn tail of about 4in (10cm). Pull the tail up through the loop with the hook.

WEAVING IN THE ENDS AFTER SEWING

Weaving in the loose ends is usually the final step in any crochet project. All the leftover yarn from sewing can sometimes seem like a lot of work. To not get overwhelmed, it is best to weave in a few of the ends as you sew the pieces together.

Step 1: Thread a large embroidery needle with the end or yarn tail, then insert the needle through the amigurumi piece and out at a location that is inconspicuous. Insert the needle underneath a few stitches along one of the rows or rounds.

Step 2: Pull the yarn slightly tight and then reverse to come back in the other direction under a few more stitches. Hide the remaining yarn tail in the amigurumi piece.

FINISHING TOUCHES

This next section will teach you the how-tos of sewing all the pieces together and adding those special details to your mythical creatures. It is the last step of completing your amigurumi so you can sit back and enjoy your accomplishments.

WHIP STITCH
Whip stitch is used to attach the body parts together.

First make sure the two pieces are pinned against each other in the location the pattern states. Thread the large embroidery needle with the leftover tail of the first piece being attached and insert the needle under the stitch of the matched-up stitch on the second piece and pull it through. Next, bring the needle back up and under both loops of the next stitch on the piece that is being attached and pull it tight. Then insert the needle under the next stitch of the second piece. Repeat the steps until both pieces are secure.

To add whip stitches to noses or cheeks using a small embroidery needle, insert the needle in the first location stated in the instructions and out at the second location. Repeat the steps until the number of whip stitches needed have been completed.

MATTRESS STITCH
This stitch is used to attach pieces together leaving the last round of dc stitches raised and exposed, creating an edging detail on the pieces.

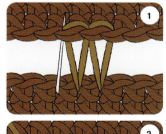

Step 1: First make sure the two pieces are pinned against each other in the location the pattern states. Thread a large embroidery needle with the leftover tail of the first piece, insert the

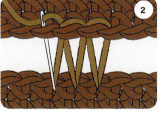

needle under the stitch post or bar of the matched-up stitch on the second piece and pull it through tightly. The stitch post or bar is the bottom part of the stitch that connects two rounds together.

Step 2: Insert the needle back through the same hole you started on the first piece and out under the next stitch post, then pull it though. Repeat the steps until both pieces are secure.

STITCHES AND TECHNIQUES

LOOP AND HOOK FOR ADDING HAIR

Full instructions are given in the steps for the Griffin's tail (see page 133).

Step 1: Fold the piece of trimmed yarn in half. Insert the crochet hook under the stitch in the round indicated in the pattern. Grab the centre of the folded piece of yarn with the crochet hook and pull it partway through the stitch, making a loop.

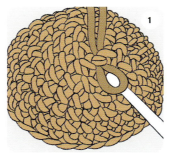

Step 2: With the crochet hook still in the loop, grab the end section of the yarn and draw it through the loop and tighten.

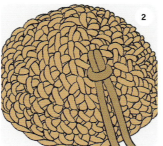

ADDING SAFETY EYES

Note that safety eyes are small and can be dangerous if removed by a small child; you may prefer to embroider the eyes instead.

Place the stem of the eye through the skipped stitch on the round indicated in the pattern. With the stem exposed on the inside of the crocheted head, firmly push the washer over the stem until it clicks into place. The tighter the washer is against the back side of the eye, the less chance your eye details will slip under them.

If you are working with curved or cup-shaped washers, make sure the open cup side of the washer is placed on the stem first. This will sink the eye into the washer and help to prevent it from falling off.

. . . .

OUTLINING THE SAFETY EYES

Safety eyes on amigurumi are usually solid black with a dull or matt finish. When crochet thread is used to outline the eyes, it gives the amigurumi realistic features by adding a sweet expression.

Step 1: Using white crochet thread, push the needle through the bottom of the head and out at the inside bottom corner of the first eye (I tend to use a smaller embroidery needle with a sharp tip for this). Then insert your needle back through the top outside corner of the eye (the diagonal corner of the eye). Pull the thread through the head and out of the same stitch or near where you entered. This adds a stripe to the lower portion of the eye. Do not pull too tight otherwise the thread may slip under the eye.

CROCHETED MYTHICAL CREATURES

Step 2: Secure this thread in place by having it come back up and circle the middle of the thread strand. Take the needle back through the bottom of the head at the starting point, tie it off and hide the thread tail inside the head. Then repeat the steps for the second eye.

Step 3: Starting with black crochet thread, push the needle through the bottom of the head and out at the inside bottom corner of the first eye. Insert your needle back through the top outside corner of the eye (diagonal corner of the eye), but a stitch away from the white thread. Pull the thread through the head and out the same stitch or near where you entered. Do not pull too tight otherwise the thread may slip under the eye.

Step 4: Secure this thread in place by having it come back up and circle the middle of the thread strand. Take the needle back through the bottom of the head at the starting point, tie it off and hide the thread tail inside the head. Then repeat the steps for the second eye.

A few of the patterns have slight adjustments on the inside corner locations for the white and black thread. Some eye outlining details will start one to two stitches over from the instructions above. This can give some of the patterns a slightly different facial expression.

ABBREVIATIONS

The patterns in this book are written in UK crochet terms.

BLO	back loop only
BOB	bobble stitch
ch	chain
cm	centimetre(s)
dc	double crochet
dc2inc	work 2 double crochet stitches into the next stitch to increase
dc2tog	work 2 double crochet stitches together to decrease
dtr	double treble
dtr2inc	work 2 double treble stitches into the next stitch to increase
FLO	front loop only
htr	half treble
htr2inc	work 2 half treble stitches into the next stitch to increase
htr2tog	work 2 half treble stitches together to decrease
in	inch(es)
m	metre(s)
MC	magic circle
POP	popcorn stitch
PUFF	puff stitch
sk	skip
sl st	slip stitch
st(s)	stitch(es)
tr	treble
tr2inc	work 2 treble stitches into the next stitch to increase
tr2tog	work 2 treble stitches together to decrease
yd	yard(s)

THE DESIGNS

MEDUSA THE GORGON

Medusa was the only mortal of the three Gorgon sisters. She was once a beautiful Greek maiden who was cursed by the goddess Athena and turned into a hideous monster with a head full of slithering snakes. Medusa was then doomed to turn into stone all those who gazed into her eyes.

Skill Level

● ● ●

Finished size

7in (18cm)

Supplies and materials

Universal Yarn Brand Bamboo Pop DK, 50% cotton, 50% bamboo (292yd/266m per 3½oz/100g): Lemongrass 133, Chocolate 152, Sundae 139, White 101, Clover 109, Lime Green 108, Bubblegum 141

Crochet thread 10:
Black and white

Hook size: 2mm

Safety eyes: ½in (12mm)

Polyester fibre filling

Embroidery needles

Sewing pins

Stitch markers

Scissors

Pipe cleaners

ARMS

Make two arms in Lemongrass colour. Work all the stitches in a round from bottom to top. Do not stuff. Wire will be added to the arms later.

Round 1: Make a MC with 6 dc (6 sts).
Round 2: (Dc2inc) 6 times (12 sts).
Rounds 3-6: Dc in each st around (12 sts).
Round 7: Dc 4, (dc2tog) twice, dc 4 (10 sts).
Rounds 8-19: Dc in each st around (10 sts).
Fasten off and hide tails inside the arms.

ONE PIECE BODY AND HEAD

Start by making two legs in Chocolate colour yarn. Work all stitches in a round from bottom to top. Stuff as you crochet.

Round 1: Make a MC with 9 dc (9 sts).
Round 2: (Dc2inc) 9 times (18 sts).
Round 3: Dc2inc, dc 6, (dc2inc) 4 times, dc 6, dc2inc (24 sts).
Round 4: FLO sl st in each st around (24 sts).
Fasten off and weave tails inside the rounds.
Attach Lemongrass colour yarn to the BLO of round 3 on the back side.
Round 5: BLO dc in each st around (24 sts).
Round 6: Dc in each st around (24 sts).
Round 7: Dc 8, (dc2tog, dc) twice, dc2tog, dc 8 (21 sts).
Round 8: Dc 7, dc2tog, dc, dc2tog, dc 7, dc2tog (18 sts).
Rounds 9-20: Dc in each st around (18 sts).
Please note: If you are on the first leg, cut the yarn and fasten off. If you are on the second leg, continue to round 21. Not everyone's tension is the same. When you connect the legs, if they are not facing perfectly front, adjust your starting dc stitch count by adding or subtracting 1–2 stitches before chaining them together.
The chain in the next round counts as a stitch.

Round 21: Dc 6 (this will move the starting stitch to ensure the legs are facing forward), ch, dc to the first leg (make sure to connect the dc, 3 stitches before where you fasten off), dc 17, dc in the back of the ch, dc 18 around 2nd leg (38 sts). The ch between the back of the legs will be the new starting stitch. Move the stitch marker to this stitch.
Round 22: Dc in each st around (38 sts).
Please note: If there is a hole visible where the two legs are joined, use an embroidery needle and the leftover yarn from attaching the legs together to sew it closed with a whip stitch.
Round 23: Dc 9, (dc2inc) twice, dc 17, (dc2inc) twice, dc 8 (42 sts).
Rounds 24-26: Dc in each st around (42 sts).
Round 27: Dc 9, (dc2tog) twice, dc 17, (dc2tog) twice, dc 8 (38 sts).
Change colour to Sundae.
Round 28: FLO dc in each st around (38 sts).
Round 29: BLO dc in each st around (38 sts).
Change colour to Lemongrass.
Round 30: BLO dc 9, dc2tog, dc 17, dc2tog, dc 8 (36 sts).
Round 31: (Dc 2, dc2tog, dc 2) 6 times (30 sts).
Rounds 32-34: Dc in each st around (30 sts).
Change colour to White.
Round 35: FLO sl st in each st around (30 sts).
Round 36: BLO dc in each st around (30 sts).
Rounds 37-39: Dc in each st around (30 sts).
Change colour to Lemongrass.
At this point, you will begin to add the arms. Remember that not everyone's tension is the same. When you add the left and right arms, if they are not parallel with the sides of the legs, add or subtract 1–2 stitches before their placement. Then adjust the starting point of the stitch marker to accommodate the extra stitches.
Round 40: BLO dc 7, dc 5 (place the first arm at the side of the body and stitch the body and arm together with these next 5 stitches. The hook will go through both the arm and the body, leaving the outside 5 stitches of the arm alone. Make sure the decreases from round 7 on the arms are facing forward), dc 11, dc 5 (place the second arm at the side of the body and stitch the body and arm together with these next 5 stitches, leaving the outside 5 stitches of the arm alone. Make sure the

decreases from round 7 on the arms are facing forward), dc 2 (30 sts).

Round 41: Dc 7, dc 5 (stitching into the 5 stitches along the outside of the arm), dc 11, dc 5 (stitching into the 5 stitches along the outside of the arm), dc 2 (30 sts).

Round 42: Dc in each st around (30 sts).

Take two pipe cleaners and twist them together to make one thick pipe cleaner. Take the two ends and twist them together to make a point. Bring the bottom centre of the pipe cleaners up to the twist. This will create two long wires that you will feed down through both of the arms. Push the wire down in the first arm and then into the second arm. This will leave the ends of the wire coming up out of the neck.

Round 43: (Dc 3, dc2tog) 6 times (24 sts).
Round 44: (Dc, dc2tog, dc) 6 times (18 sts).
Round 45: (Dc 2, dc2tog, dc 2) 3 times (15 sts).
Round 46: Dc in each st around (15 sts).

Do not cut the yarn; continue to round 47 to make the head.

HEAD

Round 47: FLO (dc 2, dc2inc, dc 2) 3 times (18 sts).
Round 48: FLO (dc, dc2inc, dc) 6 times (24 sts).
Round 49: FLO (dc 3, dc2inc) 6 times (30 sts).
Round 50: (Dc 2, dc2inc, dc 2) 6 times (36 sts).
Round 51: (Dc 5, dc2inc) 6 times (42 sts).
Round 52: (Dc 3, dc2inc, dc 3) 6 times (48 sts).
Round 53: (Dc 7, dc2inc) 6 times (54 sts).
Round 54: (Dc 4, dc2inc, dc 4) 6 times (60 sts).
Rounds 55–58: Dc in each st around (60 sts).
Round 59: Dc 33, ch, sk, dc 12, ch, sk, dc 13 (60 sts).

Please note: The chain spaces with the skip in round 59 will be where you place the safety eyes later in the pattern. The chain spaces should line up with the armpits of the doll. If they do not, adjust them left or right by a few stitches to get the correct placement, remembering to have 12 dc between each chain space.

Rounds 60–62: Dc in each st around (60 sts).
Round 63: (Dc 4, dc2tog, dc 4) 6 times (54 sts).

At this time, add the safety eyes in the chain spaces on round 59.

MEDUSA THE GORGON

Round 64: (Dc 7, dc2tog) 6 times (48 sts).
Round 65: Dc in each st around (48 sts).
Round 66: (Dc 3, dc2tog, dc 3) 6 times (42 sts).
Round 67: (Dc 5, dc2tog) 6 times (36 sts).
Round 68: (Dc 2, dc2tog, dc 2) 6 times (30 sts).
Round 69: (Dc 3, dc2tog) 6 times (24 sts).
Round 70: (Dc, dc2tog, dc) 6 times (18 sts).
Round 71: (Dc, dc2tog) 6 times (12 sts).
Round 72: (Dc, dc2tog) 4 times (8 sts).
Fasten off and weave the yarn under each of the FLO, pull tight, and hide the end inside the head.

EARS

Make two ears in Lemongrass colour yarn. Work all the stitches in a round.
Round 1: Make a MC with 9 dc (9 sts).
Fasten off and do not close the MC; leave it open with long tails to attach to the head.

SKIRT

Work in rounds and then flat rows using White colour yarn. Turn the doll upside down and attach the yarn with a sl st to the FLO of round 29 but on the right side of the doll.
Round 1: Ch, FLO dc 38, join with a sl st, ch 2 (38 sts).
Round 2: Tr in each st around, tr (in the same st as the ch sts on round 1), ch 2, turn (38 sts).
Row 3: Tr2tog, tr 36, ch 2, turn (37 sts).
Row 4: Tr in each st around, ch 2, turn (37 sts).
Row 5: Tr2tog, tr 35, ch 2, turn (36 sts).
Row 6: Tr in each st around, ch 2, turn (36 sts).
Row 7: Tr2tog, tr 34, ch 2, turn (35 sts).
Row 8: Tr in each st around, ch 2, turn (35 sts).
Row 9: Tr2tog, tr 33, ch 2, turn (34 sts).
Row 10: Tr in each st around, ch 2, turn (34 sts).
Row 11: Tr2tog, tr 32, ch 2, turn (33 sts).
Row 12: Tr in each st around, ch 2, turn (33 sts).
Row 13: Tr2tog, tr 31, ch, turn (32 sts).
Change yarn colour to Sundae.
Turn and work 32 dc along the bottom of the skirt. (Dc, ch 3, turn and sl st in the 3rd ch from hook, dc) in the corner, work 25 dc up the edge of the skirt to the waist and then 25 dc down the other side of the skirt to the starting corner. (Dc, ch 3, turn and sl st in the 3rd ch from hook, dc) in the corner, sl st to the first dc to fasten off (86 sts).

SHIRT

Work in flat rows using White colour yarn.
Attach the yarn with a dc to the FLO of round 39 but on the front right side of the doll. This will be the top round of the shirt.
After each row, ch and turn and work back the other way.
Row 1: FLO dc 12, ch, turn (12 sts).
Row 2: Dc in each st along, ch, turn (12 sts).
Row 3: Dc2tog, dc 6, htr, tr, dtr, dtr2inc, ch 2 (12 sts).
Fasten off and weave the yarn tails inside the shirt.
Flip the doll upside down and repeat rows 1–3 for the back of the shirt, starting on the same side as the front.
Row 1: FLO dc 11, ch, turn (11 sts).
Row 2: Dc in each st along, ch, turn (11 sts).
Row 3: Dc2tog, dc 5, htr, tr, dtr, dtr2inc, ch 2 (11 sts).
Fasten off, tie the two ends together and weave the yarn tails inside the shirt.

SHIRT MEDALLION

Work all stitches in a round using Sundae colour yarn.

Round 1: Make a MC with 8 dc (8 sts).

Fasten off and leave a long tail for sewing.

With an embroidery needle, sew the back of the medallion to the corner of the shirt just above the shoulder. Leaving the highest point of the shirt showing above the medallion, pinch the two sides closed and push the needle through both sides of the shirt to sew it closed. Make sure to add at least 2 whip stitches (see page 21) to ensure the medallion is sewn tightly to the shirt.

SNAKE HAIR

Work in rounds until instructed to work in chains.
Make the first set of snake hair in Clover colour yarn.

Round 1: Make a MC with 6 dc (6 sts).
Round 2: (Dc2inc) 6 times (12 sts).
Round 3: (Dc, dc2inc) 6 times (18 sts).
Round 4: (Dc, dc2inc, dc) 6 times (24 sts).

Work the next rows in chains to create the hair strands. Then sl st to the next stitch in round 4 before starting the next row. After turning and working back up the chain, work the dc stitches in the third loop (see page 12). Then the rest of the stitches need to be worked in the third loop.

Rows 1: Ch 30, turn, POP (in the 3rd ch from the hook), dc 27 up the ch, sl st (28 sts) (1 hair strand).

Rows 2–24: Ch 30, turn, POP (in the 3rd ch from the hook), dc 27 up the ch, sl st (28 sts) (23 rows of hair strands).

Fasten off and leave a long tail for sewing.

The second set of snake hair is worked starting in Clover colour yarn and then alternating between Lime Green and Clover for the hair strands.

Round 1: Make a MC with 6 dc (6 sts).
Round 2: (Dc2inc) 6 times (12 sts).
Round 3: (Dc, dc2inc) 6 times (18 sts).

Work the next part in chains to create the hair strands. Then sl st a colour change to the next st in round 3 before starting the next row.

After turning and working back up the chain, work the dc stitches in the third loop. Then the rest of the stitches need to be worked in the third loop.

Rows 1–18: Ch 30, turn, POP (in the 3rd ch from the hook), dc 27 up the ch, sl st (28 sts) (18 rows of hair strands). Fasten off and leave a long tail for sewing.

To add the snake faces and tongues, use a long piece of black embroidery thread with an embroidery needle and enter the needle underneath the pop stitch. Exit the needle out of the side of the pop stitch, and tie a knot at the bottom of the thread where it exits. Insert the needle half a stitch over from the knot and through to the other side. Tie another knot, exit the needle down through the pop stitch and tie the two ends together. Thread one of the ends out of the front of the pop stitch to act as the tongue and hide the other yarn tail inside the pop stitch. Trim the tongue to a short length. Repeat this for the rest of the pop stitches on both of the hair pieces.

ATTACHING PIECES AND ASSEMBLY

EYES

Details on how to outline the safety eyes in crochet thread can be found in the Finishing Touches section (see page 22).

NOSE AND CHEEKS

Using pins, mark the width of the nose in the centre of the face between rounds 57 and 58 and 3 stitches apart. With a small embroidery needle, enter the yarn through the side of the head to the first nose pin. Whip stitch a nose at the two pins 4–5 times. Once complete, exit the yarn back through the same stitch on the side of the head, knot the two ends, and weave the ends into the head.

Using the Bubblegum colour yarn, whip stitch or embroider a double line beginning on the round below the safety eyes, starting near the end of the safety eye and 3 stitches wide. Enter your thread through the bottom of the head and embroider the cheeks. Once finished, bring the needle back down through the head to where it entered. Knot the thread ends together and hide them within the head.

EARS

Pin the ears on the side of the head between rounds 56 and 60 with 31 stitches between the bottom of the ears along the front of the head. When pinned evenly, sew on using the leftover ends. Weave the extra tails into the head.

SANDALS

Using an embroidery needle and the Chocolate colour yarn, add the sandal ties around the legs. Enter the needle up through the bottom of the shoe underneath the outside rim. Wrap the yarn around the front of the leg and back down to the sandal on the inside of the leg. Enter the needle through the bottom of the sandal to the starting yarn tail, tie the two ends together and hide the yarn ends inside the foot.

ATTACHING THE HAIR

Match up the MC of the first larger hair piece and the MC of the head and add a pin to the top of the hair to keep it in place. Pin approximately 13 of the hair strands to the back of the head, side by side, to cover it. Adjust the hair strands as needed to fill any bare spots.

Sew the hair using an embroidery needle and the long tail left over from making the hair. Starting at the top of the hair, make a few whip stitches around a few of the stitches on the outside rounds, making sure to go through both the hair and the head to keep the hair from moving around. Next, flip the head upside down and sew the hair strands down, beginning at the pins along the back hair strands and working your way around the back of the head.

Next, match up the MC of the second smaller hair piece and the MC of the first hair piece and add a pin to the top of that hair to keep it in place as well. Then sew the smaller hair piece on using the same steps as the first hair piece. Make sure the embroidery needle goes through both hair pieces when whip stitching along the outside rounds.

Once finished, hide all the yarn tails inside the head. Then part the hair on the left side and flip it over to the right to create a styled hair look.

THE KRAKEN

The Kraken was a legendary Norse sea monster, with a gigantic body and tentacles that were said to reach up to one and a half miles in length. It terrorized sailors and fishermen through its ability to wrap its tentacles around entire ships and pull them to the depths of the dark Norwegian sea.

Skill Level

Finished size

5½in (14cm)

Supplies and materials

Universal Yarn Brand Bamboo Pop DK, 50% cotton, 50% bamboo (292yd/266m per 3½oz/100g):
Rose 104, Marmalade 118, Coral 122,
True Red 136, White 101

Crochet thread 10:
Black and white

Hook size: 2mm

Safety eyes: 9/16in (14mm)

Polyester fibre filling

Embroidery needles

Scissors

Stitch markers

Sewing pins

Pipe cleaners

HEAD

Using Rose colour yarn, work all stitches in a round from top to bottom. Stuff as you crochet.

Round 1: Make a MC with 6 dc (6 sts).
Round 2: (Dc2inc) 6 times (12 sts).
Round 3: (Dc, dc2inc) 6 times (18 sts).
Round 4: Dc in each st around (18 sts).
Round 5: (Dc, dc2inc, dc) 6 times (24 sts).
Round 6: Dc in each st around (24 sts).

Round 7: (Dc 3, dc2inc) 6 times (30 sts).
Rounds 8-9: Dc in each st around (30 sts).
Round 10: (Dc 2, dc2inc, dc 2) 6 times (36 sts).
Round 11: Dc in each st around (36 sts).
Round 12: (Dc 5, dc2inc) 6 times (42 sts).
Rounds 13-14: Dc in each st around (42 sts).
Round 15: (Dc 3, dc2inc, dc 3) 6 times (48 sts).
Rounds 16-17: Dc in each st around (48 sts).
Round 18: (Dc 7, dc2inc) 6 times (54 sts).
Round 19: (Dc 4, dc2inc, dc 4) 6 times (60 sts).
Rounds 20-21: Dc in each st around (60 sts).
Round 22: (Dc 4, dc2tog, dc 4) 6 times (54 sts).
Round 23: Dc in each st around (54 sts).
Round 24: (Dc 7, dc2tog) 6 times (48 sts).
Round 25: (Dc 3, dc2tog, dc 3) 6 times (42 sts).
Round 26: FLO (dc 3, dc2inc, dc 3) 6 times (48 sts).
Round 27: FLO (dc 7, dc2inc) 6 times (54 sts).
Rounds 28-29: Dc in each st around (54 sts).
Round 30: (Dc 4, dc2inc, dc 4) 6 times (60 sts).
Round 31: Dc 23, ch, sk, dc 12, ch, sk, dc 23 (60 sts).
Please note: The chain spaces with the skip in round 31 will be where you place the safety eyes later in the pattern.
Rounds 32-36: Dc in each st around (60 sts).
At this time, add the safety eyes in the chain spaces on round 31.
Round 37: (Dc 4, dc2tog, dc 4) 6 times (54 sts).
Round 38: (Dc 7, dc2tog) 6 times (48 sts).
Round 39: (Dc 3, dc2tog, dc 3) 6 times (42 sts).
Round 40: (Dc 5, dc2tog) 6 times (36 sts).
Round 41: (Dc 2, dc2tog, dc 2) 6 times (30 sts).
Round 42: FLO (dc 14, dc2inc) twice (32 sts).
Round 43: Dc 2, (dc2inc, dc 3) 7 times, dc2inc, dc (40 sts).
Do not cut the yarn; continue to the next set of rows to make the tentacles.

OUTER TENTACLE LEGS

The next rows will work along and then down from round 43 to create the eight legs. Each of the eight legs will consist of four combined rows. After turning, work the next dc in the second ch from the hook along the previous row going up or down for the four rows.

Row 1: Dc 2, ch 44, turn (46 sts).
Row 2: Dc2inc, dc 42 up the ch, dc in the next st on round 43, turn (45 sts).
Row 3: Dc 43, dc2inc, ch, turn (45 sts, not including turn).
Row 4: Dc, dc2inc, dc 43, dc 2 on round 43 (48 sts).
After row 4 this completes one outer tentacle leg.
Repeat rows 1–4 until there are eight tentacles.
Fasten off and weave in the yarn tails.

INNER TENTACLE LEGS

Using Marmalade colour, work in rounds until instructed to work in chains.

Round 1: Make a MC with 6 dc (6 sts).
Round 2: (Dc2inc) 6 times (12 sts).
Round 3: (Dc, dc2inc) 6 times (18 sts).
Round 4: (Dc, dc2inc, dc) 6 times (24 sts).
Round 5: (Dc 3, dc2inc) 6 times (30 sts).
Round 6: (Dc 14, dc2inc) twice (32 sts).
Round 7: (Dc2inc, dc 3) 8 times, sl st (40 sts).

The rows will work along and then down from round 7 to create the eight inner legs. Each of the eight legs will consist of four combined rows. After turning, work the next dc in the second ch from the hook along the previous row going up or down for the four rows.

Start the tentacles in Marmalade colour yarn, then change colours when instructed.

Row 1: Ch 44, turn (44 sts).
Row 2: Dc2inc, dc 42 up the ch, dc in the next st on round 7, turn (44 sts).

The next row is worked in Marmalade, with BOB stitches in Coral (colour B). Do not cut yarn (B) when working in Marmalade between the BOB stitches, but drop it and then pick it back up when instructed. Keep the yarns on the opposite (wrong) side to the BOB stitches (right side).

Row 3: Dc 2 down row 2, (BOB in colour B, dc 4) 7 times, BOB in colour B, dc 5, dc2inc, ch, turn (45 sts).
Fasten off Coral colour yarn and weave in the yarn ends. Continue Marmalade colour to the next row.
Row 4: Dc, dc2inc, dc 43, dc 4 on round 7 (46 sts).

After row 4 this completes one outer tentacle leg. Repeat rows 1–4 until there are eight tentacles. Fasten off and weave in the yarn tails.

LARGE HEAD RUFFLE

Using True Red colour yarn, work all stitches in a row. After turning, work back the other way and place the first tr in the third st from the hook.

Row 1: Ch 28, turn (28 sts).
Row 2: (Tr 4 in the same st, ch, sk) 5 times, (dtr 5 in the same st, ch, sk) 3 times, (tr 4 in the same st, ch, sk) 4 times, tr 4 in the same st (67 sts).
Fasten off and leave a long tail for attaching.

SMALL HEAD RUFFLES

Make two small ruffles in True Red colour yarn. Work all stitches in a row. After turning, work back the other way and place the first dc in the second st from the hook.

Row 1: Ch 19, turn (19 sts).
Row 2: Dc 2, (htr, ch 3, dc in the 3rd ch from hook, htr, dc 2) 3 times, htr, ch 3, dc in the 3rd ch from hook, htr, dc 2 (34 sts).
Fasten off and leave a long tail for attaching.

THE KRAKEN

ARM TENTACLES

Make two arm tentacles in Rose colour.
Work all the stitches in a round from top to bottom.
Do not stuff.
Wire will be added to the arm tentacles later.
Round 1: Make a MC with 6 dc (6 sts).
Round 2: Dc in each st around (6 sts).
Round 3: (Dc2inc) 6 times (12 sts).
Round 4: Dc in each st around (12 sts).
Round 5: (Dc, dc2inc) 6 times (18 sts).
Round 6: Dc in each st around (18 sts).
Round 7: (Dc, d2inc, dc) 6 times (24 sts).
Round 8: (Dc, dc2tog, dc) 6 times (18 sts).
Round 9: Dc 7, (dc2tog) twice, dc 7 (16 sts).
Round 10: Dc 6, (dc2tog) twice, dc 6 (14 sts).
Round 11: Dc 5, (dc2tog) twice, dc 5 (12 sts).
Rounds 12–40: Dc in each st around (12 sts).

Take two pipe cleaners, fold them in half and twist them together to make one thick pipe cleaner. Start twisting them together about 1in (2.5cm) down from the fold to the end of the pipe cleaners. There should be an oval loop at the top, making the twisted pipe cleaner look like a spoon. Bend the loop down to touch the twisted part. The doubled pipe cleaners will now be about the length of the arm tentacle. Push the looped end up the first arm tentacle until it reaches the end of the tentacle. Repeat the steps for the second arm tentacle.

Pinch the arm tentacle closed, dc through both sides with 6 dc, and close the opening (6 sts).
Fasten off and leave a long tail for attaching, then bend each of the tentacles into an S-like shape.

TOY BOAT

Using White colour yarn, work all stitches in a round.
Round 1: Make a MC with 6 dc (6 sts).
Round 2: Dc in each st around (6 sts).
Round 3: (Dc2inc) 6 times (12 sts).
Round 4: Dc in each st around (12 sts).
Round 5: (Dc, dc2inc) 6 times (18 sts).
Round 6: (Dc, d2inc, dc) 6 times (24 sts).
Rounds 7–8: Dc in each st around (24 sts).
After round 8, sl st to the first stitch on round 8.
Round 9: FLO dc in each st around (24 sts).
Round 10: (Dc 11, dc2inc) twice (26 sts).
Round 11: Dc 11, (dc2inc) twice, dc 11, (dc2inc) twice (30 sts).
Round 12: Dc 12, (dc2inc) twice, dc 13, (dc2inc) twice, dc (34 sts).

Fasten off and leave a long tail for attaching.
Fold rounds 9–12 up to overlap rounds 5–8. This creates the base of the little boat.

NOSE RIDGE

Using Rose colour yarn, work in rows.
When turning, always dc in the 2nd ch from the hook.
Row 1: Ch 15, turn (15 sts).
Row 2: Dc 14 up the ch (14 sts).
Fasten off and leave a long tail for attaching.

ATTACHING PIECES AND ASSEMBLY

EYES

Details on how to outline the safety eyes in crochet thread can be found in the Finishing Touches section (see page 22).

FACE TENTACLES

Using Coral colour yarn, work in rows.
When turning, always dc in the 2nd ch from the hook.
Row 1: Ch 31, turn (31 sts).
Row 2: Dc 30 up the ch (30 sts).
Rows 3–4: Ch 21, turn, dc 20 up the ch (20 sts).
Row 5: Ch 31, turn, dc 30 up the ch (30 sts).
Ch, then dc 8 stitches across the top of the four tentacles, creating a seam to attach the piece later in the pattern.
Fasten off and leave a long tail for attaching.

NOSE RIDGE AND FACE TENTACLES

Using pins, secure the tentacles to the front of the face with both ends of the top row between rounds 35 and 36, with 1 stitch between each safety eye and the corners of the tentacles. Pin the centre of the top row of the tentacles up between rounds 34 and 35. With an embroidery needle and the leftover yarn tail, whip stitch (see page 21) the tentacles in place. Enter the needle through the face at the corner of the tentacle and up through the first stitch before going back down through the face. Then continue whip stitching around the top row of the tentacles in a triangle fashion until it is secure. Once finished, tie the yarn ends together and hide them within the head.

THE KRAKEN

To add the nose ridge, pin it above the tentacles in a triangle form. Pin the middle between the eyes with the two sides pinned down at the corners of the tentacles. With an embroidery needle and the leftover yarn tail, whip stitch the ridge to the face. Enter the needle through the head at the corner of the ridge, then up through the first stitch and back down through the face. Continue whip stitching along the ridge until it is sewn completely. Then tie the yarn ends together and hide them within its head.

straight. Once centred, whip stitch the ruffle using an embroidery needle and the leftover yarn tail. Weave in and hide the yarn tails within the head.

The back ruffle is attached in the same way as the front ruffle. Pin it at the magic circle and end between rounds 22 and 23. When it is in position, whip stitch it to the back of the head to sew on, weave the yarn tail in, and hide it in the head.

Large ruffle

HEAD RUFFLES

Pin the large ruffle on the top of the head, with the ends pinned at round 16. The ends should be equally spaced with 20–21 stitches between each on the back of the head. When centred on the head, use an embroidery needle and whip stitch around the edge of the ruffle to attach the pieces securely. Once complete, weave in and hide the leftover tails inside the head.

The two small head ruffles will be pinned vertically on the front and back of the head, with the front ruffle centred on the head, pinned at the magic circle and ending between rounds 22 and 23. Use multiple pins to ensure that it stays

Small ruffles

LEG TENTACLES

Pair the inside and outside tentacles together, matching up all of the tentacles. Make sure both the wrong sides of each piece face each other, then use pins to keep the pieces together while you sew.

Use the crochet hook to attach the Rose colour yarn to the last stitch of row 4 of the outer tentacles. Next, dc up and around both sides of the tentacle with approximately 88 dc stitches. Make sure to put the hook through both tentacle pieces. Then dc 4 stitches through the spaces between the tentacles.

Repeat these steps to complete the eight two-layer tentacles. After completing the eight tentacles, fasten off the yarn tails and weave them in.

Slightly twist the tentacles to make them curl.

ARM TENTACLES

Flip the Kraken over and separate the eight legs tentacles in half, four near the face and the other four near the back of the head. Pin each arm in the separated tentacle space between rounds 5 and 6 of the bottom inner tentacles with the thick end of the arm cupped down. They should have about 10 stitches between the two arm tentacles. Once aligned and centred, whip stitch the arms on using an embroidery needle and the long tail left over from each piece.

Ensuring that the arm tentacles stay upright, bring the needle up through the bottom of the body and out over the last of the 4 dc stitches between the tentacles. Insert the needle under the matching stitch on round 37 of the arm tentacle. Continue to whip stitch the last 3 dc between the tentacles and round 37 of the arm tentacle until the arm is securely attached to the body. Last, bend the arm into a S-shape. When finished, weave the yarn end into the arm.

Repeat the steps to attach the second arm tentacle.

BOAT

Pin the boat to the top of one of the arm tentacles. Using the yarn tail, whip stitch 4 stitches near each of the ends of the boat, two on the front and two on the back. Bring the embroidery

needle under a stitch on the arm and then under the BLO of round 8 of the boat and back down through the top of the arm. Move the needle through the arm to the next stitch near that corner of the boat. Bring the needle up through the arm and over the closest BLO of round 8 on the boat, then back down through the arm. Continue these steps until you have the 4 whip stitches to hold the boat in place. Once finished, weave the leftover yarn tail into the arm tentacle.

CERBERUS

Cerberus, the Hound of Hades, was a ferocious three-headed dog that guarded the gates to the underworld. In Greek legend, this monstrous dog would allow the dead to cross the threshold into Hades but prevent them from leaving. If approached by the living trying to enter, it would attack them with its poisonous fangs.

Skill Level

Finished size

7½in (19cm)

Supplies and materials

Universal Yarn Brand Bamboo Pop DK, 50% cotton, 50% bamboo (292yd/266m per 3½oz/100g):
Silken 115, White 101

Crochet thread 10:
Black and white

Hook size: 2mm

Safety eyes: 9⁄16in (14mm)

Polyester fibre filling

Embroidery needles

Scissors

Stitch markers

Sewing pins

HEAD

Make three heads using Silken colour yarn, and working all stitches in a round from back to front. Stuff as you crochet.

Round 1: Make a MC with 6 dc (6 sts).
Round 2: (Dc2inc) 6 times (12 sts).
Round 3: (Dc, dc2inc) 6 times (18 sts).
Round 4: (Dc, dc2inc, dc) 6 times (24 sts).
Round 5: (Dc 3, dc2inc) 6 times (30 sts).
Round 6: (Dc 2, dc2inc, dc 2) 6 times (36 sts).
Round 7: (Dc 5, dc2inc) 6 times (42 sts).
Round 8: Dc in each st around (42 sts).
Round 9: (Dc 3, dc2inc, dc 3) 6 times (48 sts).
Round 10: Dc in each st around (48 sts).
Round 11: (Dc 7, dc2inc) 6 times (54 sts).
Rounds 12-16: Dc in each st around (54 sts).
Round 17: (Dc 7, dc2tog) 6 times (48 sts).
Round 18: Dc 17, ch, sk, dc 12, ch, sk, dc 17 (48 sts).
Please note: The chain spaces with the skip in round 18 will be where you place the safety eyes later in the pattern.
Rounds 19-20: Dc in each st around (48 sts).
Round 21: Dc 9, dc2tog, dc 9, (dc2tog, dc) twice, dc2tog, dc 9, dc2tog, dc 7, dc2tog (42 sts).
Round 22: Dc in each st around (42 sts).
Round 23: (Dc 5, dc2tog) 6 times (36 sts).
At this time, add the safety eyes in the chain spaces on round 18.
Round 24: Dc in each st around (36 sts).
Round 25: Dc 16, (dc2tog) 3 times, dc 14 (33 sts).
Round 26: Dc 16, (dc2inc) 3 times, dc 14 (36 sts).
Rounds 27-28: Dc in each st around (36 sts).
Fasten off and hide the yarn tails inside the head. Attach White coloured yarn.

Round 29: Dc in each st around (36 sts).
Round 30 (Dc 2, dc2tog, dc 2) 6 times (30 sts).
At this point, if you haven't started to stuff the head, start the stuffing now.
Round 31: (Dc 3, dc2tog) 6 times (24 sts).
Round 32: (Dc, dc2tog, dc) 6 times (18 sts).
Round 33: (Dc, dc2tog) 6 times (12 sts).
Before the last round and fastening off, add more stuffing to the snout and pack it slightly tight. This will help keep the shape of the head.
Round 34: (Dc, dc2tog) 4 times (8 sts).
Fasten off and weave the yarn under each of the FLO, then pull tight. Bring an embroidery needle down through the centre of the magic circle and out the bottom of the head. Pull slightly to flatten round 34 and hide the end inside the head.

NOSE PANEL

With White colour yarn, make three panels working in flat rows. After each row, turn and work back the other way, placing the first htr in the third st from the hook.
Row 1: Ch 31, turn (31 sts).
Rows 2-3: Htr 29, ch 2, turn (31 sts).
Row 4: Htr 29, ch, turn (30 sts).

EDGING

Top edge: dc in the 2nd st from hook, dc 10, htr 3, (tr, ch 3, dc in the 3rd ch from hook, tr in the same st), htr 3, dc 11, dc2inc in the corner.
First side: dc, htr 3, dc, dc2inc in the corner,
Bottom edge: dc 29, dc2inc in the corner.
Second side: dc, htr 3, dc, dc2inc in the corner (79 sts). Fasten off and leave a long tail for attaching.

BODY

Using Silken colour yarn, work all stitches in a round from bottom to top.
Stuff as you crochet.
Round 1: Make a MC with 6 dc (6 sts).
Round 2: (Dc2inc) 6 times (12 sts).
Round 3: (Dc, dc2inc) 6 times (18 sts).
Round 4: (Dc, dc2inc, dc) 6 times (24 sts).
Round 5: (Dc 3, dc2inc) 6 times (30 sts).
Round 6: (Dc 2, dc2inc, dc 2) 6 times (36 sts).
Round 7: (Dc 5, dc2inc) 6 times (42 sts).
Round 8: Dc in each st around (42 sts).
Round 9: (Dc 3, dc2inc, dc 3) 6 times (48 sts).
Round 10: Dc in each st around (48 sts).
Round 11: (Dc 7, dc2inc) 6 times (54 sts).
Rounds 12-24: Dc in each st around (54 sts).
Round 25: (Dc 7, dc2tog) 6 times (48 sts).
Rounds 26-29: Dc in each st around (48 sts).
Round 30: (Dc 3, dc2tog, dc 3) 6 times (42 sts).
Rounds 31-32: Dc in each st around (42 sts).
Round 33: (Dc 5, dc2tog) 6 times (36 sts).
Round 34: Dc in each st around (36 sts).
Round 35: (Dc 2, dc2tog, dc 2) 6 times (30 sts).
Round 36: (Dc 3, dc2tog) 6 times (24 sts).
Rounds 37-41: Dc in each st around (24 sts).
Rounds 42-43: Dc 7, htr 10, dc 7 (24 sts).
Fasten off and leave a long tail for attaching.

BACK LEGS

Make two legs starting in White colour yarn. Work all stitches in a round from bottom to top. Stuff as you crochet, but do not overstuff. The top portion of the leg on one side needs to be pushed flat when sewn to the body.

Round 1: Make a MC with 6 dc (6 sts).
Round 2: (Dc2inc) 6 times (12 sts).
Round 3: (Dc, dc2inc) 6 times (18 sts).
Round 4: (Dc, dc2inc, dc) 6 times (24 sts).
Round 5: Dc 9, (BOB, dc) 3 times, BOB, dc 8 (24 sts).
Rounds 6–8: Dc in each st around (24 sts).
Fasten off and hide the yarn tails inside the foot. Attach Silken colour yarn to round 8 at the fasten-off in the back of the foot.
Round 9: Dc 9, htr 8, dc 7 (24 sts).
Round 10: (Dc, dc2tog, dc) 6 times (18 sts).
Round 11: Dc 7, (dc2tog) 3 times, dc 5 (15 sts).
Round 12: Dc 7, (dc2inc) 3 times, dc 4, dc2inc (19 sts).
Round 13: Dc2inc, dc 7, dc2inc, dc 3, dc2inc, dc 6 (22 sts).
Round 14: Dc 11, (dc2inc) twice, dc 9 (24 sts).
Round 15: (Dc 3, dc2inc) 6 times (30 sts).
Round 16: (Dc 2, dc2inc, dc 2) 6 times (36 sts).
Round 17: (Dc 5, dc2inc) 6 times (42 sts).
Rounds 18–19: Dc in each st around (42 sts).
Round 20: (Dc 5, dc2tog) 6 times (36 sts).
Round 21: (Dc 2, dc2tog, dc 2) 6 times (30 sts).
Round 22: Dc in each st around (30 sts).
Round 23: (Dc 3, dc2tog) 6 times (24 sts).
Round 24: Dc in each st around (24 sts).
Round 25: (Dc, dc2tog, dc) 6 times (18 sts).
Round 26: (Dc, dc2tog) 6 times (12 sts).
Round 27: (Dc, dc2tog) 4 times (8 sts).
Fasten off and weave the yarn under each of the FLO, pull tight, and leave a long tail for attaching.

ARMS

Make two arms in White colour yarn. Work all stitches in a round from bottom to top. Stuff as you crochet, but only until round 25, leaving the last few rounds without stuffing.

Round 1: Make a MC with 6 dc (6 sts).
Round 2: (Dc2inc) 6 times (12 sts).
Round 3: (Dc, dc2inc) 6 times (18 sts).
Round 4: (Dc, dc2inc, dc) 6 times (24 sts).
Round 5: Dc 9, (BOB, dc) 3 times, BOB, dc 8 (24 sts).
Rounds 6–8: Dc in each st around (24 sts).
Fasten off and hide the yarn tails inside the foot. Attach Silken coloured yarn to round 8 at the fasten-off in the back of the foot.
Round 9: Dc in each st around (24 sts).
Round 10: Dc 9, (dc2tog, dc) twice, dc2tog, dc 7 (21 sts).
Round 11: Dc2tog, dc 19 (20 sts).
Rounds 12–29: Dc in each st around (20 sts).
Pinch the arms closed; if your seam is not parallel with the bobble stitches on the foot, add or subtract 1–2 stitches. Dc through both sides with 10 dc and close the opening (10 sts).
Fasten off and leave a long tail for attaching.

EARS

Make six ears in Silken colour yarn.
Work all the stitches in a round from top to bottom.
Do not stuff.
Round 1: Make a MC with 5 dc (5 sts).
Round 2: (Dc2inc) 5 times (10 sts).
Round 3: Dc in each st around (10 sts).
Round 4: (Dc, dc2inc) 5 times (15 sts).
Round 5: Dc in each st around (15 sts).
Round 6: (Dc, dc2inc, dc) 5 times (20 sts).
Round 7: Dc in each st around (20 sts).
Round 8: (Dc 3, dc2inc) 5 times (25 sts).
Round 9: Dc in each st around (25 sts).
Round 10: Tr 13, FLO dc 12 (25 sts).
Round 11: Tr 13, dc 12 (25 sts).
Rounds 12-13: Dc in each st around (25 sts).
Round 14: (Dc 3, dc2tog) 5 times (20 sts).
Round 15: Dc in each st around (20 sts).
Round 16: (Dc, dc2tog, dc) 5 times (15 sts).
Pinch the ear closed; if the trebles are not centred, add or subtract 1–2 stitches.
Dc through both sides with 7 dc and close the opening (7 sts).
Fasten off and leave a long tail for attaching.

TAIL

Using Silken colour yarn, work all the stitches in a round from top to bottom. Stuff as you crochet.
Round 1: Make a MC with 6 dc (6 sts).
Round 2: Dc in each st around (6 sts).
Round 3: (Dc, dc2inc, dc) twice (8 sts).
Round 4: Dc in each st around (8 sts).

Round 5: Dc 3, (dc2inc) twice, dc 3 (10 sts).
Round 6: Dc in each st around (10 sts).
Round 7: Dc 4, (dc2inc) twice, dc 4 (12 sts).
Rounds 8-9: Dc in each st around (12 sts).
Round 10: Dc2tog, dc 4, dc2inc, dc 5 (12 sts).
Round 11: Dc in each st around (12 sts).
The next rounds will have sl sts. Make sure to work them with a loose tension.
Rows 12-13: Htr 5, FLO sl st 7 (12 sts).
Row 14: Htr 7 (leaving the other 5 sts unworked) (7 sts).
Fasten off and leave a long tail for attaching.

ATTACHING PIECES AND ASSEMBLY

EYES

Details on how to outline the safety eyes in crochet thread are found in the Finishing Touches section (see page 22).

CERBERUS

NOSE PANEL AND DETAILS

Using pins, secure the nose piece horizontally along the top of the nose with the point between the safety eyes on round 20 of the head and 4 stitches between the safety eyes and the panel. The bottom edge of the panel should end at the front of the nose, lapping two white rounds. Leave the sides of the panel hanging below the nose on either side. Make sure they are even before sewing the next step.

Next, with an embroidery needle and the leftover yarn tail, mattress stitch (see page 21) the panel in place. First, the long yarn end will need to weave through the back of the nose panel with a few stitches to match up where the lower part of the nose and the panel meet. Use mattress stitch along the top edge of the nose panel until it is attached to the face.

Once the top edge is attached, weave the yarn end through the nose to the stitch on the second white round parallel to the last mattress stitch. Repeat the mattress stitch along the bottom edge of the panel to attach the nose panel completely. When finished, weave in the yarn end and hide it within the head. Repeat these steps for the other two heads.

To create a small triangle nose, mark the nose with three pins. For the top corners, place two pins above the last round of the nose panel, separated by 4 htr stitches and evenly spaced, straight down from the point between the safety eyes. The last pin is placed three rounds above the ending magic circle on the front of the muzzle and centred between the other two pins. Using black crochet thread and a small embroidery needle, enter the needle through the bottom of the head and then out at the bottom pin. Embroider a line to each pin, ensuring the nose keeps its shape. From there, whip stitch the triangle in a fan-like shape, working from one side to the other, filling in the spaces between each threaded line. Once finished, outline the top of the nose with a few whip stitches (see page 21). Bring the needle down through the head, tie the thread ends together, and hide them within its head. Repeat these steps for the other two heads.

CROCHETED MYTHICAL CREATURES

EARS

Pin the ears on the back side of the head between rounds 7 and 8 with 4–5 stitches between the seam of the ears and bend forward. When pinned evenly, whip stitch the ears around the seventh round using the leftover yarn tails and an embroidery needle, keeping the ears upright instead of lying down. Weave the extra tails into the head once the ears are secured. Repeat these steps for the other two heads.

LEGS AND ARMS

Tilt the body forward with the htr from the last round at the front, and pin the flat portion of the legs to the sides of the body starting between rounds 25 and 26. At the widest part of the legs, leave about 16 stitches between them on the front and back of the body. With the legs pinned, the feet should be down and parallel to the surface. If the body is sitting, whip stitch using an embroidery needle around the large thigh part of the legs only. If not, take this time to adjust the legs up or down to ensure a good sitting position.

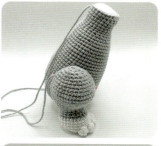

CERBERUS

Add 1–2 extra whip stitches to the inside of the foot and round 9 of the body to keep the legs secure. When finished, weave in the ends.

Pin the arms against the legs in the space between the top of the legs and the open neck portion of the body between rounds 34 and 35. Note that the seam of the arms will be at an angle and not aligned with the rows because of the tilted position of the body. Leaving about 7 stitches between the tops of the arms, add an extra pin to the inside of the leg near the feet to keep them in place for sewing. If they are even, touching the surface and the body is still sitting, whip stitch the arms to the body using an embroidery needle. If not, adjust the arms up or down to ensure a good placement.

Add 2–3 whip stitches to the back of the arms near the top seam to secure the legs against the body. Also do this at the inside of the foot and round 12 of the body, keeping the arms secure. When the arms are in place and stable, weave in the ends.

HEAD AND BODY

Before attaching the first head to the body, use pins to ensure the placement. You want the back of the neck to match up between rounds 12 and 13 of the back of the head and centred. Make sure that the nose is centred between the arms. Once aligned and centred, whip stitch the pieces together in a circle using an embroidery needle and the long tail left over from the body. When finished, weave in the end.

Pin the second and third heads to the body on the side of the neck below the first head with the chins touching the tops of the arms. Once the other heads are even, cut a long piece of Silken colour yarn to sew the pieces together. With an embroidery needle, use 4 whip stitches to attach the second head to the first at round 12. Then weave the embroidery needle through the first head out at round 12 near the third head. Attach the third head to the first with 4 whip stitches. When finished, weave in the yarn end in the head to hide it.

Secure the two heads to the arms using the embroidery needle by sewing the bottom of the chin at round 28 before the white rounds and the top of the arms with 4 whip stitches. When finished, weave the yarn end in the head to hide it.

TAIL

The tail should be pinned to get the correct placement before sewing. It should be attached on the lower back between rounds 6 and 7 and ending between rounds 10 and 11, centred with about 9 stitches between the tail and the feet. Make sure that the htrs on the last round are on the bottom of the tail. Once in place, sew the tail using an embroidery needle and the leftover yarn tail to whip stitch it onto the back. Then weave the end in the body to hide it.

CERBERUS

DJINN

The djinn is a supernatural spirit found worldwide, but mostly in Arabic mythology and Islamic culture. Djinns are said to be made from smokeless fire and can shape-shift into different forms, inhabiting objects to stay hidden from human sight. They are neither good nor evil but possess many magical abilities and may have the power to grant wishes.

Skill Level

Finished size

8½in (22cm)

Supplies and materials

Universal Yarn Brand Bamboo Pop DK, 50% cotton, 50% bamboo (292yd/266m per 3½oz/100g): Quartz 138, Winter Squash 129, Fuchsia 123, Royal 116, Sundae 139

Crochet thread 10:
Black and white

Hook size: 2mm

Safety eyes: ½in (12mm)

Polyester fibre filling

Embroidery needles

Sewing pins

Stitch markers

Scissors

Small clear plastic hairbands or ties

Pipe cleaners

ARMS

Make two arms in Quartz colour yarn.
Work all the stitches in a round from bottom to top.
Do not stuff.
Wire will be added to the arms later.

Round 1: Make a MC with 6 dc (6 sts).
Round 2: (Dc2inc) 6 times (12 sts).
Rounds 3-6: Dc in each st around (12 sts).
Round 7: Dc 4, (dc2tog) twice, dc 4 (10 sts).
Rounds 8-19: Dc in each st around (10 sts).
Fasten off and hide tails inside the arms.

ONE PIECE BODY AND HEAD

Start by making two legs in Quartz colour yarn.
Work all stitches in a round from bottom to top.
Stuff as you crochet.
Round 1: Make a MC with 9 dc (9 sts).
Round 2: (Dc2inc) 9 times (18 sts).
Round 3: Dc2inc, dc 6, (dc2inc) 4 times, dc 6, dc2inc (24 sts).
Rounds 4-6: Dc in each st around (24 sts).
Round 7: Dc 8, (dc2tog, dc) twice, dc2tog, dc 8 (21 sts).
Round 8: Dc 8, dc2tog, dc, dc2tog, dc 6, dc2tog (18 sts).
Round 9: Dc 7, (dc2tog) twice, dc 6, dc2inc (17 sts).
Round 10: Dc 8, dc2inc, dc 8 (18 sts).
Rounds 11-23: Dc in each st around (18 sts).
Please note: If you are on the first leg, cut the yarn and fasten off. If you are on the second leg, continue to Round 24. Not everyone's tension is the same. When you connect the legs, if they are not facing perfectly front, adjust your starting dc stitch count by adding or subtracting 1-2 stitches before chaining them together.
The chain in the next round counts as a stitch.
Round 24: Dc 6 (this will move the starting stitch to ensure the legs are facing forward), ch, dc to the first leg (make sure to connect the dc 3 stitches before where you fasten off), dc 17, dc in the back of the ch, dc 18 around 2nd leg (38 sts). The ch between the back of the legs will be the new starting stitch.
Round 25: Dc in each st around (38 sts).
Please note: If there is a hole visible where the two legs are joined, use an embroidery needle and the leftover yarn from attaching the legs together to sew it closed with a whip stitch.
Round 26: Dc 9, (dc2inc) twice, dc 17, (dc2inc) twice, dc 8 (42 sts).
Rounds 27-29: Dc in each st around (42 sts).
Round 30: Dc 9, (dc2tog) twice, dc 17, (dc2tog) twice, dc 8 (38 sts).
Change colour to Winter Squash on the last dc.
Round 31: FLO sl st in each st around (38 sts).
Round 32: BLO dc 9, dc2tog, dc 17, dc2tog, dc 8 (36 sts).
Round 33: (Dc 2, dc2tog, dc 2) 6 times (30 sts).
Round 34: Dc in each st around (30 sts).
Change colour to Quartz.
Round 35: BLO dc in each st around (30 sts).
Rounds 36-41: Dc in each st around (30 sts).
At this point, you will begin to add the arms. Remember that not everyone's tension is the same. When you add the left and right arms, if they are not parallel with the sides of the legs, add or subtract 1-2 stitches before their placement. Then adjust the starting point of the stitch marker to accommodate the extra stitches.
Round 42: Dc 7, dc 5 (place the first arm at the side of the body and stitch the body and arm together with the next 5 stitches. The hook will go through both the arm and the body, leaving the outside 5 stitches of the arm alone. Make sure the decreases from round 7 on the arms are facing forward), dc 11, dc 5 (place the second arm at the side of the body and stitch the body and arm together with the next 5 stitches, leaving the outside 5 stitches of the arm alone. Make sure the decreases from round 7 on the arms are facing forward), dc 2 (30 sts).
Round 43: Dc 7, dc 5 (stitching the 5 stitches along the outside of the arm), dc 11, dc 5 (stitching the 5 stitches along the outside of the arm), dc 2 (30 sts).
Round 44: Dc in each st around (30 sts).

Take two pipe cleaners and twist them together to make one thick pipe cleaner. Take the two ends and twist them together to make a point. Bring the bottom centre of the pipe cleaners up to the twist. This will create two long wires that you will feed down through both of the arms. Push the wire down in the first arm and then into the second arm. This will leave the ends of the wire coming up out of the neck.

Round 45: (Dc 3, dc2tog) 6 times (24 sts).
Round 46: (Dc, dc2tog, dc) 6 times (18 sts).
Round 47: (Dc 2, dc2tog, dc 2) 3 times (15 sts).
Round 48: Dc in each st around (15 sts).
Do not cut the yarn and continue to round 49 to make the head.

HEAD
Round 49: FLO (dc 2, dc2inc, dc 2) 3 times (18 sts).
Round 50: FLO (dc, dc2inc, dc) 6 times (24 sts).
Round 51: FLO (dc 3, dc2inc) 6 times (30 sts).
Round 52: (Dc 2, dc2inc, dc 2) 6 times (36 sts).
Round 53: (Dc 5, dc2inc) 6 times (42 sts).
Round 54: (Dc 3, dc2inc, dc 3) 6 times (48 sts).
Round 55: (Dc 7, dc2inc) 6 times (54 sts).
Round 56: (Dc 4, dc2inc, dc 4) 6 times (60 sts).
Rounds 57–60: Dc in each st around (60 sts).
Round 61: Dc 30, ch, sk, dc 12, ch, sk, dc 16 (60 sts).
Please note: The chain spaces with the skip in round 61 will be where you place the safety eyes later in the pattern. The chain spaces should line up with the armpits of the doll. If they do not, adjust them left or right by a few stitches to get the correct placement, remembering to have 12 dc between each chain space.

DJINN

Rounds 62–64: Dc in each st around (60 sts).
Round 65: (Dc 4, dc2tog, dc 4) 6 times (54 sts).
At this time, add the safety eyes in the chain spaces on round 61.
Round 66: (Dc 7, dc2tog) 6 times (48 sts).
Round 67: Dc in each st around (48 sts).
Round 68: (Dc 3, dc2tog, dc 3) 6 times (42 sts).
Round 69: (Dc 5, dc2tog) 6 times (36 sts).
Round 70: (Dc 2, dc2tog, dc 2) 6 times (30 sts).
Round 71: (Dc 3, dc2tog) 6 times (24 sts).
Round 72: (Dc, dc2tog, dc) 6 times (18 sts).
Round 73: (Dc, dc2tog) 6 times (12 sts).
Round 74: (Dc, dc2tog) 4 times (8 sts).
Fasten off and weave the yarn under each of the FLO, pull tight, and hide the end inside the head.

LOINCLOTHS

Make two loincloths in Fuchsia colour yarn.
Starting with a long yarn tail, work in rows.
After each row, turn and work back the other way, placing the first tr in the third st from the hook.

FRONT LOINCLOTH
Row 1: Ch 10, turn (10 sts).
Rows 2–20: Tr in each st along, ch 2, turn (8 sts).
Fasten off and weave the last yarn tail inside the loincloth but leaving the first starting yarn tail to attach the pieces later.

BACK LOINCLOTH
Row 1: Ch 10, turn (10 sts).
Rows 2–10: Tr in each st along, ch 2, turn (8 sts).
Fasten off and weave the last yarn tail inside the loincloth but leaving the first starting yarn tail to attach the pieces later.

EARS

Make two ears in Quartz colour yarn.
Work all the stitches in a round.
Round 1: Make a MC with 10 dc, ch turn (10 sts).
Round 2: Dc 3, htr, tr, ch 3, turn, dc in the 3rd ch from hook, tr (in the same st as the last tr), htr, dc 3 (13 sts).
Fasten off and close the MC, leaving a long tail to attach to the head.

HAIR

Using Royal colour yarn, work in rounds until instructed to work in chains.

Round 1: Make a MC with 6 dc (6 sts).
Round 2: (Dc2inc) 6 times (12 sts).

Work the next part in chains. This will create the hair strands. Then sl st to the next st on round 2 before starting the next row.

Rows 1–6: Sl st, ch 86 turn, dc 85 up the ch, sl st (85 sts) (6 rows of hair strands).

Fasten off and leave a long tail for sewing.

HEADBAND

Using Sundae colour yarn, work in flat rows.
After the ch row, turn and work back the other way, placing the first dc in the second st from the hook.

Row 1: Ch 25, turn (25 sts).
Row 2: Dc in each st along (24 sts).

Fasten off and leave a long tail to attach to the head.

SMALL BANDS

Make four small bands in Sundae colour yarn. Starting with a long yarn tail, work in rows.
After the ch row, turn and work back the other way, placing the first dc in the second st from the hook.

Row 1: Ch 14, turn (14 sts).
Row 2: Dc in each st along (13 sts).

Fasten off and leave a long tail to attach the pieces to the arms and hair later.

ATTACHING PIECES AND ASSEMBLY

EYES

Details on how to outline the safety eyes in crochet thread are found in the Finishing Touches section (see page 22).

NOSE

Using pins, mark the width of the nose in the centre of the face between rounds 58 and 59 and three stitches apart. With a small embroidery needle, enter the yarn through the side of the head to the first nose pin. Whip stitch (see page 21) a nose at the two pins 4–5 times. Once complete, exit the yarn back through the same stitch on the side of the head, knot the two ends, and weave the ends into the head.

EARS

Pin the ears on the side of the head between rounds 58 and 62 with 7 stitches between the bottom of the ears and the safety eyes. When pinned evenly, use an embroidery needle and the leftover yarn ends to whip stitch 3 stitches on the bottom of the ear to the head. Then bring the needle up through the centre magic circle of the ear and then back through the top stitches of the magic circle and whip stitch the middle of the ear to the head. Weave the extra tails into the head.

ATTACHING THE HAIR

Match up the MC of the hair piece and the MC of the head and add a pin to the top of the hair to keep it in place. Sew the hair using the embroidery needle and the long tail leftover from making the hair. Starting at the top of the hair, make a few whip stitches around a few of the stitches on the outside rounds, making sure to go through both the hair and the head to keep the hair from moving around.

Flip the doll upside down and, starting at the top of the doll's head, group the six hair strands in pairs. Then, with the strands paired, braid them all the way to the bottom. Wrap a clear plastic hairband or tie around the bottom strands to secure the ends.

Next, circle the headband around the base of the hair piece and add a pin to the back of the band to keep it in place. Then sew the ends of the hairband together with a few whip stitches and an embroidery needle making it one piece. Once the hairband is sewn together, whip stitch the bottom of the hairband to the head. When finished, hide all the yarn tails inside the head.

Add two of the small bands around the braid: one at the bottom around the clear hair band that is securing the hair pieces, and the other in the centre of the braid. Make sure to use the embroidery needle to whip stitch each of the small bands' ends together to close them around the hair. Once finished, tie the yarn ends in a knot under each of the bands and hide the ends within them.

LOINCLOTHS

Using pins, secure the top of the front loincloth with the long leftover tails to underneath the FLO of round 31 of the front of the body. This is the start of the Winter Squash colour on the waist. Make sure the loincloth is centred on the body before sewing. With an embroidery needle and the leftover yarn tail of the loincloth, whip stitch the top of the loincloth underneath the FLO of round 31. Then weave the yarn tail inside the body. Repeat the steps for the second, short back loincloth on the back of the body.

SMALL BANDS

Add the last two of the small bands around each of the wrists. Using an embroidery needle, whip stitch each of the small bands' ends together to close them around the wrists. Once finished, tie the yarn ends in a knot under each of the bands and leave two long yarn tails hanging from each of the bands.

THE FAUN

Fauns, originating from Roman and Greek mythology, were wise and gentle creatures that were part human and part goat. They were spirits of the forests and fields who protected sacred places and brought balance to nature while symbolizing growth and fertility. They were said to have a great sense of direction and could lead travellers on their merry way.

Skill Level

Finished size

7½in (19cm)

Supplies and materials

Universal Yarn Brand Bamboo Pop DK, 50% cotton, 50% bamboo (292yd/266m per 3½oz/100g):
Seashell 145, Chocolate 152, Hickory 151, Apricot Slush 135, Cream 102, Almond 148, Sunny 113, Bubblegum 141 (optional)

Crochet thread 10:
Black and white

Hook size: 2mm

Safety eyes: ½in (12mm)

Polyester fibre filling

Embroidery needles

Sewing pins

Stitch markers

Scissors

Pipe cleaners

Pet grooming brush (optional)

ARMS

Make two arms in Seashell colour yarn.
Work all the stitches in a round from bottom to top.
Do not stuff.
Wires will be added to the arms later.

Round 1: Make a MC with 6 dc (6 sts).
Round 2: (Dc2inc) 6 times (12 sts).
Rounds 3-6: Dc in each st around (12 sts).
Round 7: Dc 4, (dc2tog) twice, dc 4 (10 sts).
Rounds 8-19: Dc in each st around (10 sts).
Fasten off and hide tails inside the arms.

ONE PIECE BODY AND HEAD

Start by making two hooves in Chocolate colour yarn.
Work all stitches in a round from bottom to top.
Stuff as you crochet.
Round 1: Make a MC with 9 dc (9 sts).
Round 2: (Dc2inc) 9 times (18 sts).
Round 3: BLO dc in each st around (18 sts).
Rounds 4-5: Dc in each st around (18 sts).
Fasten off and weave tails inside the rounds.
Attach Hickory colour yarn to the BLO of round 5 on the back side.
Round 6: BLO dc in each st around (18 sts).
Rounds 7-11: Dc in each st around (18 sts).
Round 12: Dc 5, FLO (dc, dc2inc) 4 times, dc 5 (22 sts).
Round 13: Dc 5, FLO (dc2inc, dc 2) twice, FLO (dc 2, dc2inc) twice, dc 5 (26 sts).
Rounds 14-16: Htr 3, dc 20, htr 3 (26 sts).
Round 17: Dc, dc2tog, dc 20, dc2tog, dc (24 sts).
Rounds 18-20: Dc in each st around (24 sts).
Please note: If you are on the first leg, cut the yarn and fasten off. If you are on the second leg, continue to Round 21. Not everyone's tension is the same. When you connect the legs, if they are not facing perfectly front with the knees forward, adjust your starting dc stitch count by adding or subtracting 1-2 stitches before chaining them together.
The chain in the next round counts as a stitch.
Round 21: Dc 6 (this will move the starting stitch to the side of the leg to ensure the legs are facing forward), ch, dc to the first leg (make sure to connect the dc, 3 stitches to the right from where you fasten off), dc 23, dc in the back of the connecting ch, dc 24 around 2nd leg (50 sts).
The chain between the back of the legs will be the new starting stitch.
Round 22: Dc in each st around (50 sts).
Please note: If there is a hole visible where the two legs are joined, use an embroidery needle and a short length of yarn to sew it closed with a whip stitch (see page 21).
Rounds 23-25: Dc in each st around (50 sts).
Round 26: Dc 23, (dc2tog) twice, dc 23 (48 sts).
Round 27: (Dc 3, dc2tog, dc 3) 6 times (42 sts).
Round 28: Dc 6, dc2tog, dc 4, dc2tog, dc 15, dc2tog, dc 4, dc2tog, dc 5 (38 sts).
Fasten off and weave tails inside the rounds.
Attach Seashell colour yarn to the first dc.
Round 29: BLO dc in each st around (38 sts).
Round 30: Dc in each st around (38 sts).
Round 31: Dc 9, dc2tog, dc 17, dc2tog, dc 8 (36 sts).
Round 32: (Dc 2, dc2tog, dc 2) 6 times (30 sts).
Rounds 33-35: Dc in each st around (30 sts).
At this point, you will begin to add the arms. Remember that not everyone's tension is the same. When you add the left and right arms, if they are not parallel with the sides of the legs, add or subtract 1-2 stitches before their placement. Then adjust the starting point of the stitch marker to accommodate the extra stitches.
Round 36: Dc 6, dc 5 (place the first arm at the side of the body and stitch the body and arm together with the next 5 stitches. The hook will go through both the arm and the body, leaving the outside 5 stitches of the arm alone. Make sure the decreases from round 7 on the arms are facing forward), dc 10, dc 5 (place the second arm at the side of the body and stitch the body and arm together with the next 5 stitches, leaving the outside 5 stitches of the arm alone. Make sure the decreases from round 7 on the arms are facing forward), dc 4 (30 sts).

Round 37: Dc 6, dc 5 (stitching the 5 stitches along the outside of the arm), dc 10, dc 5 (stitching the 5 stitches along the outside of the arm), dc 4 (30 sts).

Round 38: Dc in each st around (30 sts).

Take two pipe cleaners and twist them together to make one thick pipe cleaner. Take the two ends and twist them together to make a point. Bring the bottom centre of the pipe cleaners up to the twist. This will create two long wires that you will feed down through both of the arms. Push the wire down in the first arm and then into the second arm. This will leave the ends of the wire coming up out of the neck.

Round 39: (Dc 3, dc2tog) 6 times (24 sts).
Round 40: (Dc, dc2tog, dc) 6 times (18 sts).
Round 41: (Dc 2, dc2tog, dc 2) 3 times (15 sts).
Round 42: Dc in each st around (15 sts).

Do not cut the yarn and continue to round 43 to make the head.

HEAD

Round 43: FLO (dc 2, dc2inc, dc 2) 3 times (18 sts).
Round 44: FLO (dc, dc2inc, dc) 6 times (24 sts).
Round 45: FLO (dc 3, dc2inc) 6 times (30 sts).
Round 46: (Dc 2, dc2inc, dc 2) 6 times (36 sts).
Round 47: (Dc 5, dc2inc) 6 times (42 sts).
Round 48: (Dc 3, dc2inc, dc 3) 6 times (48 sts).
Round 49: (Dc 7, dc2inc) 6 times (54 sts).
Round 50: (Dc 4, dc2inc, dc 4) 6 times (60 sts).
Rounds 51-54: Dc in each st around (60 sts).
Round 55: Dc 26, ch, sk, dc 12, ch, sk, dc 20 (60 sts).
Please note: The chain spaces with the skip in round 55 will be where you place the safety eyes later in the pattern. The chain spaces should line up with the armpits of the doll. If they do not, adjust them left or right by a few stitches to get the correct placement, remembering to have 12 dc between each chain space.
Rounds 56-58: Dc in each st around (60 sts).
Round 59: (Dc 4, dc2tog, dc 4) 6 times (54 sts).
At this time, add the safety eyes in the chain spaces on round 55.
Round 60: (Dc 7, dc2tog) 6 times (48 sts).
Round 61: Dc in each st around (48 sts).
Round 62: (Dc 3, dc2tog, dc 3) 6 times (42 sts).
Round 63: (Dc 5, dc2tog) 6 times (36 sts).
Round 64: (Dc 2, dc2tog, dc 2) 6 times (30 sts).
Round 65: (Dc 3, dc2tog) 6 times (24 sts).
Round 66: (Dc, dc2tog, dc) 6 times (18 sts).
Round 67: (Dc, dc2tog) 6 times (12 sts).
Round 68: (Dc, dc2tog) 4 times (8 sts).
Fasten off and weave the yarn under each of the FLO, pull tight, and hide the end inside the head.

EARS

INNER EAR

Make two inner ear pieces in Apricot Slush colour yarn. Work all the stitches in a round.
Round 1: Make a MC with 6 dc (6 sts).
Round 2: (Dc2inc) 6 times (12 sts).
Round 3: (Dc, dc2inc) 6 times (18 sts).
Round 4: (Dc, dc2inc, dc) 6 times (24 sts).
Fasten off and hide the tails inside the inner ear.

OUTSIDE EAR

Make two outer ear pieces in Seashell colour yarn. Work all the stitches in a round.

Round 1: Make a MC with 6 dc (6 sts).
Round 2: (Dc2inc) 6 times (12 sts).
Round 3: (Dc, dc2inc) 6 times (18 sts).
Round 4: (Dc, dc2inc, dc) 6 times (24 sts).
Round 5: Dc in each st around (24 sts).

Place both the inside and outside parts of the ear together. Make sure both the wrong sides of each piece are facing each other. Dc the next round through both pieces of the ear, making them into one complete ear.

Round 6: Dc in each st around (24 sts).

Pinch the ear closed and dc across only the next 3 stitches connecting both sides, closing the top of the ear and creating a small seam.
Fasten off and leave a long tail for attaching.

HORNS

Make two horns in Cream colour yarn.
Work all the stitches in a round from top to bottom. Do not stuff.
Wire will be added after the last round.

Round 1: Make a MC with 4 dc (4 sts).
Round 2: (Dc, dc2inc) twice (6 sts).
Round 3: Dc in each st around (6 sts).
Round 4: Dc 2, (dc2inc) twice, dc 2 (8 sts).
Round 5: Dc in each st around (8 sts).
Round 6: Dc 3, (dc2inc) twice, dc 3 (10 sts).
Round 7: Dc in each st around (10 sts).
Round 8: Dc 4, (dc2inc) twice, dc 4 (12 sts).
Rounds 9–10: Dc in each st around (12 sts).
Round 11: Dc2tog, dc 3, (dc2inc) twice, dc 3, dc2tog (12 sts).
Rounds 12–13: Dc in each st around (12 sts).
Round 14: Dc2tog, dc 3, (dc2inc) twice, dc 3, dc2tog (12 sts).
Rounds 15–16: Dc in each st around (12 sts).
Round 17: Dc2tog, dc 3, (dc2inc) twice, dc 3, dc2tog (12 sts).
Rounds 18–19: Dc in each st around (12 sts).
Round 20: Dc2tog, dc 3, (dc2inc) twice, dc 3, dc2tog (12 sts).
Rounds 21–22: Dc in each st around (12 sts).
Round 23: Dc2tog, dc 3, (dc2inc) twice, dc 3, dc2tog (12 sts).
Rounds 24–25: Dc in each st around (12 sts).
Round 26: Dc2tog, dc 3, (dc2inc) twice, dc 3, dc2tog (12 sts).
Rounds 27–28: Dc in each st around (12 sts).
Round 29: Dc2tog, dc 3, (dc2inc) twice, dc 3, dc2tog (12 sts).
Rounds 30–31: Dc in each st around (12 sts).

Fasten off and leave a long tail for attaching.
Fold one pipe cleaner twice and push inside the horn to the end. Make sure the wire is not sticking out of the horn.

SHIRT

FRONT PANELS

Make two panels working in flat rows using Almond colour yarn.

When turning, always tr in the 3rd stitch or chain from the hook, working back up the other way.

Row 1: Ch 20, turn (20 sts).
Rows 2-3: Tr 18, ch 2, turn (18 sts).
Rows 4-5: Tr 10, ch 2, turn (10 sts).
Row 6: Tr in each st along (10 sts).

Fasten off and leave a long tail for attaching.

BACK PANEL

Work in flat rows using Almond colour yarn.

When turning, always tr in the 2nd stitch or chain from the hook, working back up the other way.

Row 1: Ch 20, turn (20 sts).
Rows 2-7: Tr 18, ch 2, turn (18 sts).
Row 8: Tr in each st along (18 sts).

Fasten off and leave a long tail for attaching.

Whip stitch (see page 21) is used to attach the three pieces of the shirt. Place the side panels next to the back panel with the rows of stitches on all three pieces in a vertical position, ensuring the grain of the stitches are all working in the same direction. The left panel should be in an L-shape, with the last row next to the bottom left section of the back panel and the right panel reversed like a backward L on the other side. Using an embroidery needle, whip stitch the sides to the back panel, then whip stitch the top of the side panels to the top of the back panel. This will complete the shirt. Weave in any leftover ends within the shirt.

HAIR

Using Sunnny colour yarn, work in rounds until instructed to work in chains.

Round 1: MC with 6 dc (6 sts).
Round 2: (Dc2inc) 6 times (12 sts).
Round 3: (Dc, dc2inc) 6 times (18 sts).
Round 4: (Dc, dc2inc, dc) 6 times (24 sts).

Work the next rows in chains to create the hair strands. When crocheting in a chain, after turning, work the first dc stitch in the second chain from the hook. Then sl st to the next stitch in round 4 before starting the next row.

Rows 1–13: Ch 26, turn, dc 25 up the ch, sl st (25 sts) (13 rows of hair strands).
Rows 14–24: Ch 13, turn, dc 12 up the ch, sl st (12 sts) (11 rows of hair strands).

Fasten off and leave a long tail for sewing.

TAIL

Using Hickory colour yarn, work all the stitches in a round from top to bottom. Do not stuff.

Round 1: Make a MC with 4 dc (4 sts).
Round 2: (Dc, dc2inc) twice (6 sts).
Round 3: (Dc, dc2inc, dc) twice (8 sts).
Round 4: Dc in each st around (8 sts).
Round 5: (Dc 3, dc2inc) twice (10 sts).

Pinch the tail closed, dc through both sides with 5 dc, and close the opening (5 sts).

Fasten off and leave a long tail for attaching.

FAUN

ATTACHING PIECES AND ASSEMBLY

EYES
Details on how to outline the safety eyes in crochet thread can be found in the Finishing Touches section (see page 22).

NOSE AND CHEEKS
Using pins, mark the width of the nose in the centre of the face between rounds 53 and 54 and three stitches apart. With a small embroidery needle, enter the yarn through the side of the head to the first nose pin. Whip stitch a nose at the two pins 4–5 times. Once complete, exit the yarn back through the same stitch on the side of the head, knot the two ends, and weave the ends into the head.

Optional Cheeks: Using the Bubblegum colour yarn, whip stitch or embroider a double line beginning on the round below the safety eyes, starting near the end of the safety eye and 3 stitches wide. Enter your thread through the bottom of the head and embroider the cheeks. Once finished, bring the needle back down through the head to where it entered. Knot the thread ends together and hide them within the head.

EARS
Pin the ears on the side of the head between rounds 54 and 55 with 7 stitches between the seam of the ears and the safety eyes. When pinned evenly, sew on using the leftover ends. Weave the extra tails into the head.

ATTACHING THE HAIR
Match up the MC of the first larger hair piece and the MC of the head and add a pin to the top of the hair to keep it in place. Pin approximately 13 of the hair strands to the back of the head, side by side, to cover it. Adjust the hair strands as needed to fill any bare spots.

Sew the hair using an embroidery needle and the long tail left over from making the hair. Starting at the top of the hair, make a few whip stitches around a few of the stitches on the outside rounds, making sure to go through both the hair and the head to keep the hair from moving around. Next, flip the head upside down and sew the hair strands down with a whip stitch, beginning at the pins along the back hair strands and working your way around the back of the head.

Leave the shorter hair strand loose until after the horns are placed and sewn onto the head.

HORNS

Pin the horns 4 rounds above the safety eyes, starting at round 61. Leave 6–7 stitches between the horns on round 62 and place them slightly forward on the centre of the head. Make sure to have the horns pointing upwards and to the outside above the ears. Then attach the horns with an embroidery needle by whip stitching around the edge to attach the piece securely. Once complete, weave in and hide the leftover tails inside the horns.

ATTACHING SMALL STRANDS OF HAIR

Pin the smaller hair strands around the horns to your liking. Then, using an embroidery needle and the long tail left over from making the hair, sew each strand to the head with a whip stitch. Once finished, hide the leftover tail inside the head.

TAIL

Like all other parts, the tail will need to be pinned to get the right placement before sewing. It should be sewn on the FLO of round 28 of the back of the body at the colour change. Once centred on the back, using whip stitches, sew the tail on with the small embroidery needle, then weave in the end.

BRUSHING (OPTIONAL)

With a pet grooming brush, gently brush the Hickory colour legs to make them slightly fuzzy. Avoid brushing the colours that make up the hooves and the body to keep the fuzzy section distinct.

CHINESE DRAGON

The dragon symbolizes many different things in Chinese culture and folklore. It has a long serpent-like body, scaly skin and a majestic presence, and holds great power, strength and good fortune. It is often believed to control the earthly elements, and is known to ward off evil spirits.

Skill Level

Finished size

9in (18cm)

Supplies and materials

Universal Yarn Brand Bamboo Pop DK, 50% cotton, 50% bamboo (292yd/266m per 3½oz/100g): True Red 136, Emerald 117, Marmalade 118

Crochet thread 10: Black and white

Hook size: 2mm

Safety eyes: 9/16in (14mm)

Polyester fibre filling

Embroidery needles

Scissors

Sewing pins

Stitch markers

HEAD

Using True Red colour yarn, work all stitches in a round from top to bottom.

Stuff as you crochet.

Round 1: Make a MC with 6 dc (6 sts).
Round 2: (Dc2inc) 6 times (12 sts).
Round 3: (Dc, dc2inc) 6 times (18 sts).
Round 4: (Dc, dc2inc, dc) 6 times (24 sts).
Round 5: (Dc 3, dc2inc) 6 times (30 sts).
Round 6: (Dc 2, dc2inc, dc 2) 6 times (36 sts).
Round 7: (Dc 5, dc2inc) 6 times (42 sts).
Round 8: (Dc 3, dc2inc, dc 3) 6 times (48 sts).
Round 9: (Dc 7, dc2inc) 6 times (54 sts).
Round 10: (Dc 4, dc2inc, dc 4) 6 times (60 sts).
Round 11: (Dc 9, dc2inc) 6 times (66 sts).
Round 12: (Dc 5, dc2inc, dc 5) 6 times (72 sts).
Round 13: Dc 48, leaving 24 dc sts unworked (48 sts).

Place a stitch marker on 2 unworked stitches: stitch 49 and stitch 72 of round 12. This will mark the neck section to work later in the pattern. The next set of rounds will create the head only by working around the 48 stitches of round 13. Fold the piece in half and work round 14.

Round 14: Dc in each st around (48 sts).
Round 15: (Dc 7, dc2inc) 6 times (54 sts).
Round 16: Dc in each st around (54 sts).
Round 17: (Dc 7, dc2tog) 6 times (48 sts).
Round 18: Dc 16, ch, sk, dc 16, ch, sk, dc 14 (48 sts).

Please note: The chain spaces with the skip in round 18 will be where you place the safety eyes later in the pattern.

Round 19: Dc in each st around (48 sts).
Round 20: Dc 9, dc2tog, dc 10, (dc2tog, dc) twice, dc2tog, dc 10, dc2tog, dc 5, dc2tog (42 sts).
Round 21: Dc in each st around (42 sts).
Round 22: (Dc 5, dc2tog) 6 times (36 sts).

At this time, add the safety eyes in the chain spaces on round 18.

Round 23: Dc in each st around (36 sts).
Round 24: Dc 17, (dc2tog) 3 times, dc 13 (33 sts).
Round 25: Dc 17, (dc2inc) 3 times, dc 13 (36 sts)
Round 26: (Dc 2, dc2tog, dc 2) 6 times (30 sts).
Round 27: Dc in each st around (30 sts).

At this point, if you haven't started to stuff the head, start the stuffing now.

Round 28: (Dc 3, dc2tog) 6 times (24 sts).
Round 29: (Dc, dc2tog, dc) 6 times (18 sts).
Round 30: (Dc, dc2tog) 6 times (12 sts).

Before the last round and fastening off, add more stuffing to the snout and pack it slightly tight. This will help maintain the shape of the head.

Round 31: (Dc, dc2tog) 4 times (8 sts).

Fasten off and weave the yarn under each of the FLO, then pull tight. Bring an embroidery needle down through the centre of the magic circle and out the bottom of the head. Pull slightly to flatten round 31 and hide the end inside the head.

NECK AND BODY

Attach the True Red colour yarn to the first stitch of the open neck from round 13, and leave a long starting tail. Work all stitches in a round from right to left.

Stuff as you crochet, making sure to stuff the bottom of the head and the opening of the top of the neck. The hole left over from connecting the two pieces will be closed when the body is finished.

Rounds 14-19: Dc in each st around (24 sts).
Round 20: (Dc 3, dc2inc) 6 times (30 sts).
Rounds 21-43: Dc in each st around (30 sts).

The next four rows will be worked on the front of the body. This will allow the front of the dragon to curve. If it is not curved, adjust your starting dc stitch on round 44 by adding or subtracting 1-2 stitches to centre the dc stitches.

When turning, do not chain but dc in the 2nd stitch from the hook, working back the other way.

Row 44: Dc 17, turn, leaving the other sts unworked (17 sts). In the next row, your stitches will pass the starting stitch before reaching the 24th dc.

Row 45: Dc 24, turn, leaving the other sts unworked (24 sts).

For rows 46-51, the last stitch in each row will be left unworked before turning.

Row 46: Dc 22, turn (22 sts).
Row 47: Dc 20, turn (20 sts).
Row 48: Dc 18, turn (18 sts).
Row 49: Dc 16, turn (16 sts).
Row 50: Dc 14, turn (14 sts).
Row 51: Dc 12, turn (12 sts).

Next will be a round: do not turn after the 11 dc stitches and work the 7 dc stitches down the side of the rows. Then continue around the opening of the neck to make a full round.

Round 52: Dc 11, dc 7 down the 1st side, dc 3, dc2inc, dc 2, dc 7 up the 2nd side (32 sts).

The starting stitch will now be moved to the first stitch on the previous row. Make sure to move the stitch marker.

CHINESE DRAGON

Round 53: Dc 5, dc2inc, dc 12, (dc2inc, dc 2) twice, dc2inc, dc 7 (36 sts).
Rounds 54-58: Dc in each st around (36 sts).
Round 59: (Dc 2, dc2tog) 3 times, dc 8, (dc2inc, dc 2) twice, dc2inc, dc 9 (36 sts).
Rounds 60-61: Dc in each st around (36 sts).
Round 62: (Dc 2, dc2tog) 3 times, dc 8, (dc2inc, dc 2) twice, dc2inc, dc 9 (36 sts).
Rounds 63-64: Dc in each st around (36 sts).
Round 65: Dc 3, dc2tog, dc, dc2tog, dc 28 (34 sts).
Rounds 66-67: Dc in each st around (34 sts).
Round 68: Dc 13, dc2tog, dc 14, dc2tog, dc 3 (32 sts).
Round 69: Dc in each st around (32 sts).
Round 70: Dc 5, dc2tog, dc 13, dc2tog, dc 10 (30 sts).
Round 71: Dc in each st around (30 sts).
Round 72: Dc2tog, dc 13, dc2tog, dc 13 (28 sts).
Round 73: Dc in each st around (28 sts).
Round 74: Dc 8, dc2tog, dc 13, dc2tog, dc 3 (26 sts).
Round 75: Dc in each st around (26 sts).
Round 76: Dc2tog, dc 11, dc2tog, dc 11 (24 sts).
Round 77: Dc in each st around (24 sts).
Round 78: Dc 18, (dc2tog) twice, dc 2 (22 sts).
Round 79: Dc in each st around (22 sts).
Round 80: Dc 18, (dc2tog) twice (20 sts).
Round 81: Dc in each st around (20 sts).
Round 82: Dc 16, (dc2tog) twice (18 sts).
Rounds 83-85: Dc in each st around (18 sts).
Round 86: Dc 14, (dc2tog) twice (16 sts).
Rounds 87-89: Dc in each st around (16 sts).
Round 90: Dc 12, (dc2tog) twice (14 sts).
Rounds 91-93: Dc in each st around (14 sts).
Round 94: Dc 10, (dc2tog) twice (12 sts).
Rounds 95-100: Dc in each st around (12 sts).
Round 101: (Dc, dc2tog) 4 times (8 sts).
Fasten off and weave the yarn under each of the FLO, then pull tight and hide the yarn end in the tail.
Please note: There will be a hole visible where the head and neck connect; use an embroidery needle and the leftover yarn from starting round 14 or cut a new yarn piece about 5in (12.5cm) long to sew it closed with 3-4 whip stitches (see page 21).

ARMS

Make two arms in True Red colour yarn, working all stitches in a round from bottom to top.
Stuff as you crochet.
Round 1: Make a MC with 6 dc (6 sts).
Round 2: (Dc2inc) 6 times (12 sts).
Round 3: Dc 3, (BOB, dc 2) 3 times (12 sts).
Round 4: Dc in each st around (12 sts).
Round 5: (Dc2inc) 3 times, dc 2, (dc2tog) twice, dc 3 (13 sts).
Round 6: Dc in each st around (13 sts).
Round 7: Dc 2, dc2inc, dc 10 (14 sts).
Rounds 8-11: Dc in each st around (14 sts).
Rounds 12-13: Dc 2, htr 5, FLO dc 7 (14 sts).

Round 14: Dc 2, dc2tog, dc, dc2tog, dc 3, (dc2inc) twice, dc 2 (14 sts).
Rounds 15–19: Dc in each st around (14 sts).
Round 20: Dc 4, leaving the other sts unworked (4 sts). Pinch the arms closed. If the seam is still not centred with the middle toe on the paw after the last 4 sts, add or subtract 1–2 stitches.
Dc through both sides with 7 dc and close the opening (7 sts).
Fasten off, leaving a long tail for attaching.

Round 15: Dc 3, dc2inc, dc 2, dc2inc, dc 2, dc2tog, dc, dc2tog, dc (15 sts).
Rounds 16–20: Dc in each st around (15 sts).
Round 21: Dc 7, leaving the other sts unworked (7 sts). Pinch the legs closed. If the seam is still not centred with the middle toe on the paw after the last 7 sts, add or subtract 1–2 stitches.
Dc through both sides with 7 dc and close the opening (7 sts).
Fasten off, leaving a long tail for attaching.

LEGS

Make two legs in True Red colour yarn, working all stitches in a round from bottom to top.
Stuff as you crochet.
Round 1: Make a MC with 6 dc (6 sts).
Round 2: (Dc2inc) 6 times (12 sts).
Round 3: Dc 3, (BOB, dc 2) 3 times (12 sts).
Round 4: Dc in each st around (12 sts).
Round 5: (Dc2inc) 3 times, dc 2, (dc2tog) twice, dc 3 (13 sts).
Rounds 6–8: Dc in each st around (13 sts).
Round 9: Dc 2, dc2inc, dc 5, dc2inc, dc 4 (15 sts).
Rounds 10–12: Dc in each st around (15 sts).
Rounds 13–14: FLO dc 9, htr 5 in both loops, FLO dc (15 sts).

EYE FINS

Make two fins in Emerald colour yarn, working all the stitches in a flat row.
All stitches in row 2 need to be worked in the third loop (see page 12).
After each row, turn and work back the other way, placing the first dc in the second st from the hook.
Row 1: Ch 7, turn (7 sts).
Row 2: Dc, (tr, ch 3, dc in the 3rd ch from hook, tr in the same st), dc, (tr, ch 3, dc in the 3rd ch from hook, tr in the same st), dc 2, ch 6, turn, sl st in the 2nd ch from hook, dc, htr, tr 2, tr in the 1st starting ch (28 sts).
Fasten off and leave a long tail for attaching.

CHINESE DRAGON

MOUTH AND CHEEKS

The mouth and cheeks are made in two pieces using Marmalade colour yarn. First, work in rounds until instructed to change.

Round 1: Make a MC with 6 dc (6 sts).
Round 2: BLO (Dc2inc) 6 times (12 sts).
Round 3: BLO (Dc, dc2inc) 6 times (18 sts).

Next, work all stitches in a row, turn and work back the other way, placing the first dc in the second st from the hook.
All stitches in row 2 need to be worked in the third loop (see page 12). This keeps the chain from twisting.

Row 1: Ch 31, turn (31 sts).
Row 2: Dc 11, PUFF, ch 2, dc in the next ch after the PUFF st, dc 4, PUFF, ch 2, dc in the next ch after the PUFF st, dc 10, sl st to the next st on round 3 of the cheek (34 sts).

Fasten off and leave a long tail for attaching.
For the second part, make another cheek only.

Round 1: Make a MC with 6 dc (6 sts).
Round 2: BLO (Dc2inc) 6 times (12 sts).
Round 3: BLO (Dc, dc2inc) 6 times (18 sts).

Fasten off and leave a long tail for attaching. Attach the end of the chain to the fasten-off stitch of the second cheek with a whip stitch using an embroidery needle.

WHISKERS

Using Marmalade colour yarn, make two whiskers working all the stitches in a flat row.

All stitches in row 2 need to be worked in the third loop (see page 12). This keeps the whiskers from curling.

After the first row, turn and work back the other way, placing the first dc in the second st from the hook.

Row 1: Ch 31, turn (31 sts).
Row 2: Dc in each st across (30 sts).

Fasten off and leave a long tail for attaching.

BELLY PLATE

Make the piece in Marmalade colour yarn, working all the stitches in a flat row.

Row 1: Ch 10, turn (10 sts).
Row 2: Htr in the 2nd ch from hook, htr 3, (htr 3) in the same st, htr 4, ch 2, turn (11 sts).

When turning after each row, place the first decrease in the third st from the hook. Work the FLO and the BLO in each st across.

Row 3: FLO htr2tog, htr 3, (htr 3) in the same st, htr 3, htr2tog, ch 2, turn (11 sts).
Row 4: BLO htr2tog, htr 3, (htr 3) in the same st, htr 3, htr2tog, ch 2, turn (11 sts).
Row 5: FLO htr2tog, htr 3, (htr 3) in the same st, htr 3, htr2tog, ch 2, turn (11 sts).

Row 6: BLO htr2tog, htr 3, (htr 3) in the same st, htr 3, htr2tog, ch 2, turn (11 sts).
Row 7: FLO htr2tog, htr 3, (htr 3) in the same st, htr 3, htr2tog, ch 2, turn (11 sts).
Row 8: BLO htr2tog, htr 3, (htr 3) in the same st, htr 3, htr2tog, ch 2, turn (11 sts).
Row 9: FLO htr2tog, htr 3, (htr 3) in the same st, htr 3, htr2tog, ch 2, turn (11 sts).
Row 10: BLO htr2tog, htr 3, (htr 3) in the same st, htr 3, htr2tog, ch 2, turn (11 sts).
Row 11: FLO htr2tog, htr 3, (htr 3) in the same st, htr 3, htr2tog, ch 2, turn (11 sts).
Row 12: BLO htr2tog, htr 3, (htr 3) in the same st, htr 3, htr2tog, ch 2, turn (11 sts).
Row 13: FLO htr2tog, htr 3, (htr 3) in the same st, htr 3, htr2tog, ch 2, turn (11 sts).
Row 14: BLO htr2tog, htr 3, (htr 3) in the same st, htr 3, htr2tog, ch 2, turn (11 sts).
Row 15: FLO htr2tog, htr 3, (htr 3) in the same st, htr 3, htr2tog, ch 2, turn (11 sts).
Row 16: BLO htr2tog, htr 3, (htr 3) in the same st, htr 3, htr2tog, ch 2, turn (11 sts).
Row 17: FLO htr2tog, htr 3, (htr 3) in the same st, htr 3, htr2tog, ch (11 sts).
Turn and work approximately 70 dc around the complete edge of the belly piece (70 sts).
Fasten off and leave a long tail for attaching.

BACK FIN

Make a long back fin in Emerald colour yarn.
All stitches in row 2 need to be worked in the third loop (see page 12). Work all stitches in a row, turn and work back the other way, placing the first dc in the 2nd st from the hook.
Row 1: Ch 84, turn (84 sts).
Row 2: Dc 2, (tr, ch 3, dc in the 3rd ch from hook, tr in the same st, dc 3) 12 times, dc 3, (tr, ch 3, dc in the 3rd ch from hook, tr in the same st, dc 3) 7 times, tr, ch 3, dc in the 3rd ch from hook, tr in the same st, dc (183 sts) (20 points).
Fasten off and leave a long tail for attaching.

TAIL FINS

Make a fin in Emerald colour yarn, working all the stitches in a flat row.
All stitches in row 2 need to be worked in the 3rd loop. After each row, turn and work back the other way, placing the first dc in the 2nd st from the hook.
Row 1: Ch 14, turn (14 sts).
Row 2: Sl st, dc, (tr, ch 3, dc in the 3rd ch from hook, tr in the same st, dc 3) twice, tr, ch 3, dc in the 3rd ch from hook, tr in the same st, dc, sl st (28 sts) (3 points).
Fasten off and leave a long tail for attaching.

CHINESE DRAGON

ATTACHING PIECES AND ASSEMBLY

EYES
Details on how to outline the safety eyes in crochet thread can be found in the Finishing Touches section (page 22).

pin the right cheek under the other safety eye on the same rounds where the left eye is located. Make sure the cheeks and chains are even on both sides before moving on to the next steps.

With an embroidery needle and the leftover yarn tail, mattress stitch (see page 21) around the left cheek to sew in place. Then move the needle up to the first stitch on the top of the chain and continue the mattress stitch technique along the chain until you reach the right cheek to attach it to the face. Once the mouth and the cheeks are attached, weave the end into the head.

MOUTH AND CHEEKS
Before whip stitching the pieces, follow the next steps to pin the mouth and cheeks to the face. Pin the puff stitches 6 to 7 rounds down from the safety eyes and 4 stitches apart. Then pin the left cheek built onto the chain, under the safety eyes between rounds 16 and 17 and ending at rounds 22 and 23. There should be 2–3 rounds between the top of the cheek and the bottom of the safety eyes. Positioning the cheek on these rounds of the face will make the chain curved. Next,

EYE FINS
The eye fins should be pinned above the safety eyes starting with the smaller of the three points first. Begin between rounds 18 and 19 on the inside of each safety eye, working up and around with the longer point ending between rounds 15 and 16, near the cheek. Once the placement is correct, whip stitch them onto the head using an embroidery needle and the leftover yarn end. When finished, weave the ends into the head.

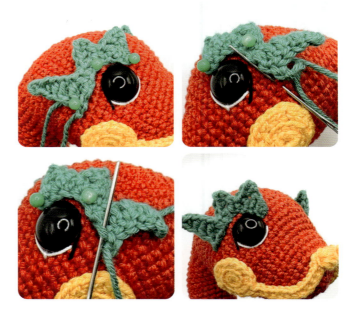

BELLY PLATE

Pin the belly to the front of the body beginning between rounds 19 and 20 and ending around round 54 with the pattern in a V-shape pointing down. Use an embroidery needle with the long leftover yarn ends to mattress stitch the belly to the front of the body. When you have finished attaching the piece, weave the ends into the body.

LEGS

To get the dragon to stand up straight, pin both the arms and legs on before sewing. This ensures that the weight distribution on the front of the dragon's body is even. Pin the top seam of the arms to the sides of the body between rounds 22 and 27 with the first stitch of the seam up against the belly panel and angled down towards the tail. Next, pin the legs to the sides of the body between rounds 40 and 46 past the curve of the lower body and angled onto the tail. Leave about 3 stitches between the top of the seam and the belly panel. Once the dragon is standing upright, start whip stitching the seams of the arms and legs in place with an embroidery needle and the leftover yarn end of each of the pieces. If not, take this time to adjust the legs up or down to ensure a good standing position before sewing.

Add 2–3 whip stitches to the back of the arms and legs near the top seam to secure the pieces against the body. Then add 2 whip stitches to the htr stitches to keep the legs sewn close to the body. When the pieces are sewn in place and stable, weave in all the ends.

BACK FIN

Pin the long back fin to the top of the head starting between rounds 20 and 21, then down the centre of the back to the end of the tail near round 98. The 3 dc stitches between the 12 points and the last 8 points should be pinned at the curve where the body becomes the tail. Use multiple pins to ensure the piece is in the centre of the body before sewing. Whip stitch on with an embroidery needle and the extra yarn tails. Weave in the extra yarn end after the back fin is sewn in place.

TAIL FIN

The tail fin should be pinned around the outside of the end of the tail. The ends of the fin should be about 3–4 stitches away from the end of the back fin. Whip stitch on with an embroidery needle and the extra yarn ends. When secure, weave in all the extra yarn ends into the tail.

WHISKERS

Pin the whiskers to the outside of the puff stitches but 1 stitch over on the mouth and cheek details. Attach them using an embroidery needle and the extra yarn ends by adding 2–3 whip stitches to the mouthpiece. When secure, weave in all the yarn ends into the head.

CHINESE DRAGON

NESSIE THE LOCH NESS MONSTER

This creature from Scottish folklore is said to inhabit Loch Ness, a large freshwater lake near Inverness. It is described as a serpent-like monster that is very large and green in colour with an elongated neck that has been seen to stick out of the water. Perhaps Nessie's best-known image is a famous black and white photograph from 1934.

Skill Level

Finished size

9in (18cm)

Supplies and materials

Universal Yarn Brand Bamboo Pop DK, 50% cotton, 50% bamboo (292yd/266m per 3½oz/100g): Lime Green 108, Cream 102, Tropical Green 124, Marmalade 118, Bubblegum 141

Crochet thread 10: Black and white

Hook size: 2mm

Safety eyes: 9/16in (14mm)

Polyester fibre filling

Embroidery needles

Scissors

Stitch markers

Sewing pins

Pipe cleaners

HEAD

Using Lime Green colour yarn, work all stitches in a round from top to bottom.
Stuff as you crochet.

Round 1: Make a MC with 5 dc (5 sts).
Round 2: (Dc2inc) 5 times (10 sts).
Round 3: (Dc, dc2inc) 5 times (15 sts).
Round 4: (Dc, dc2inc, dc) 5 times (20 sts).
Round 5: (Dc, dc2inc) 10 times (30 sts).
Round 6: (Dc 2, dc2inc, dc 2) 6 times (36 sts).
Round 7: (Dc 5, dc2inc) 6 times (42 sts).
Round 8: (Dc 3, dc2inc, dc 3) 6 times (48 sts).
Round 9: (Dc 7, dc2inc) 6 times (54 sts).
Round 10: (Dc 4, dc2inc, dc 4) 6 times (60 sts).
Round 11: (Dc 9, dc2inc) 6 times (66 sts).
Round 12: (Dc 5, dc2inc, dc 5) 6 times (72 sts).
Round 13: Dc 48, leaving 24 dc sts unworked (48 sts).
Place a stitch marker on the 2 unworked stitches, stitch 49 and stitch 72 of round 13. This will mark the neck section to work later in the pattern. The next set of rounds will create the head only, by working around the 48 stitches of round 13. Fold the piece in half and work round 14.
Round 14: Dc in each st around (48 sts).
Round 15: (Dc 7, dc2inc) 6 times (54 sts).
Round 16: Dc in each st around (54 sts).
Round 17: (Dc 7, dc2tog) 6 times (48 sts).
Round 18: Dc 11, ch, sk, dc 24, ch, sk, dc 11 (48 sts).
Please note: The chain spaces with the skip in round 18 will be where you place the safety eyes later in the pattern.
Round 19: Dc in each st around (48 sts).
Round 20: Dc 9, dc2tog, dc 8, (dc2tog, dc) twice, dc2tog, dc 8, dc2tog, dc 9, dc2tog (42 sts).
Round 21: Dc in each st around (42 sts).
Round 22: (Dc 5, dc2tog) 6 times (36 sts).
At this time, add the safety eyes in the chain spaces on round 18.
Round 23: Dc in each st around (36 sts).
Round 24: Dc 16, (dc2tog) 3 times, dc 14 (33 sts).
Round 25: Dc 16, (dc2inc) 3 times, dc 14 (36 sts)
Round 26: (Dc 2, dc2tog, dc 2) 6 times (30 sts).
Round 27: Dc in each st around (30 sts).
At this point, if you haven't started to stuff the head, start the stuffing now.

Round 28: (Dc 3, dc2tog) 6 times (24 sts).
Round 29: (Dc, dc2tog, dc) 6 times (18 sts).
Round 30: (Dc, dc2tog) 6 times (12 sts).
Before the last round and fastening off, add more stuffing to the snout and pack it fairly tight to help retain the shape of the head.
Round 31: (Dc, dc2tog) 4 times (8 sts).
Fasten off and weave the yarn under each of the FLO, then pull tight. Bring an embroidery needle down through the centre of the magic circle and out the bottom of the head. Pull slightly to flatten round 31 and hide the yarn end inside.

NECK AND BODY

Join the Lime Green yarn to the first stitch of the 24 unworked stitches and work in a round. Make sure to leave a long tail to sew the hole between the head and the neck later.
Stuff as you crochet.
Rounds 14–17: Dc in each st around (24 sts).
With an embroidery needle and the starting yarn tail, close the hole on the neck with 2–3 whip stitches (see page 21). Hide the leftover end inside the neck.
Rounds 18–24: Dc in each st around (24 sts).
The htr stitches in the next few rounds need to be centred on the front of the neck. If they are not, adjust your starting dc stitch on round 24 by adding or subtracting 1–2 stitches to centre the htr stitches.
Round 25: Dc 21, htr 3 (24 sts).
Rounds 26–27: Htr 11, dc 10, htr 3 (24 sts).
On rounds 28–30, make sure to have loose tension when working the slip stitches. This will help you to get the hook underneath both loops when working the next rounds.
Rounds 28–30: Htr 11, sl st 10, htr 3 (24 sts).
Round 31: Dc in each st around (24 sts).
Round 32: (Dc 5, dc2inc) 4 times (28 sts).
Round 33: Dc 15, dc2inc, dc 6, dc2inc, dc 5 (30 sts).
Round 34: Dc 16, dc2inc, dc 7, dc2inc, dc 5 (32 sts).
Round 35: Dc 17, dc2inc, dc 8, dc2inc, dc 5 (34 sts).
Round 36: Dc 18, dc2inc, dc 9, dc2inc, dc 5 (36 sts).
The increases for rounds 37–42 should be on the top of the body to create a small hump. As instructed before, if they are not, adjust your starting dc stitch on round 37 by adding or subtracting 1–2 stitches to centre the increases.
Round 37: Dc 23, (dc2inc) twice, dc 11 (38 sts).
Round 38: Dc 23, dc2inc, dc 2, dc2inc, dc 11 (40 sts).
Round 39: Dc 24, dc2inc, dc 4, dc2inc, dc 10 (42 sts).
Round 40: Dc 27, (dc2inc) twice, dc 13 (44 sts).
Round 41: Dc 27, dc2inc, dc 2, dc2inc, dc 13 (46 sts).
Round 42: Dc 27, dc2inc, dc 4, dc2inc, dc 13 (48 sts).
Rounds 43–44: Dc in each st around (48 sts).
Round 45: Dc 6, dc2tog, dc 22, dc2tog, dc 16 (46 sts).
Round 46: Dc 16, dc2tog, dc 24, dc2tog, dc 2 (44 sts).
Round 47: Dc 27, (dc2tog) twice, dc 13 (42 sts).
Round 48: Dc in each st around (42 sts).
Round 49: (Dc 5, dc2tog) 6 times (36 sts).
Rounds 50–51: Dc in each st around (36 sts).
Make sure to pack the bottom of the neck at the curve and the body tightly with stuffing. The piece should be firm.

NESSIE THE LOCH NESS MONSTER

Round 52: (Dc 2, dc2tog, dc 2) 6 times (30 sts).
Rounds 53-54: Dc in each st around (30 sts).
Round 55: (Dc 3, dc2tog) 6 times (24 sts).
Rounds 56-59: Dc in each st around (24 sts).
Round 60: (Dc, dc2tog, dc) 6 times (18 sts).
Rounds 61-66: Dc in each st around (18 sts).
Do not add stuffing past round 66. A folded pipe cleaner will be added to the tail later in the pattern.
Round 67: (Dc, dc2tog) 6 times (12 sts).
Rounds 68-81: Dc in each st around (12 sts).
Round 82: (Dc, dc2tog) 4 times (8 sts).
Round 83: Dc in each st around (8 sts).
Take a pipe cleaner, fold it in half, then half once more and twist it from one end to the other to create one thick pipe cleaner. Fold ¾in (2cm) of the end down to thicken one end. The pipe cleaner should be about 2¼in (6cm) in total length now. Push the end with the last fold all the way up the tail until it reaches the stuffing.
Fasten off and weave the yarn under each of the FLO, pull tight and hide the end inside the tail.

UNDERBELLY
Work the underbelly in flat rows using Cream colour yarn. After each row, turn and work back the other way, placing the first htr in the 2nd st from the hook.
Row 1: Ch 4, turn (4 sts).
Row 2: Htr 3, ch, turn (3 sts).
Row 3: Htr2inc, htr, htr2inc, ch, turn (5 sts).
Row 4: Htr 2, htr2inc, htr 2, ch turn (6 sts).
Row 5: Htr2inc, htr 4, htr2inc, ch, turn (8 sts).
Rows 6-14: Htr in each st along, ch, turn (8 sts).
Row 15: Htr2inc, htr 6, htr2inc, ch, turn (10 sts).
Row 16: Htr in each st along, ch, turn (10 sts).
Row 17: Htr2inc, htr 8, htr2inc, ch, turn (12 sts).
Row 18: Htr in each st along, ch, turn (12 sts).
Row 19: Htr2inc, htr 10, htr2inc, ch, turn (14 sts).
Row 20: Htr in each st along, ch, turn (14 sts).
Row 21: Htr2inc, htr 12, htr2inc, ch, turn (16 sts).
Row 22: Htr in each st along, ch, turn (16 sts).
Row 23: Htr2tog, htr 12, htr2tog, ch, turn (14 sts).
Row 24: Htr2tog, htr 10, htr2tog, ch, turn (12 sts).
Row 25: Htr2tog, htr 8, htr2tog, ch, turn (10 sts).
Row 26: Htr in each st along, ch, turn (10 sts).
Row 27: Htr2tog, htr 6, htr2tog, ch, turn (8 sts).
Rows 28-29: Htr in each st along, ch, turn (8 sts).
Row 30: Htr2tog, htr 4, htr2tog, ch, turn (6 sts).
Rows 31-32: Htr in each st along, ch, turn (6 sts).
Row 33: Htr2tog, htr 2, htr2tog, ch, turn (4 sts).
Row 34: (Htr2tog) twice, ch, turn (2 sts).
Row 35: Htr2tog, ch (1 st).

EDGING
Turn and work approximately 102 dc around the complete edge of the underbelly piece. Once finished, fasten off, leaving an extra-long tail to attach it to the body (102 sts).

FINS

Make four fins in Lime Green colour yarn, working all the stitches in a round from bottom to top.
Do not stuff.
Round 1: Make a MC with 6 dc (6 sts).
Round 2: Dc in each st around (6 sts).
Round 3: (Dc2inc) 6 times (12 sts).
Rounds 4-5: Dc in each st around (12 sts).
Round 6: (Dc, dc2inc) 6 times (18 sts).
Rounds 7-8: Dc in each st around (18 sts).
Round 9: (Dc, dc2inc, dc) 6 times (24 sts).
Rounds 10-12: Dc in each st around (24 sts).
Round 13: (Dc, dc2tog, dc) 6 times (18 sts).
Round 14: Dc in each st around (18 sts).
Round 15: Dc 5, (dc2tog) 4 times, dc 5 (14 sts).
Rounds 16-18: Dc in each st around (14 sts).
Pinch the fin closed, dc through both sides with 7 dc to close the opening (7 sts).
Fasten off and leave a long tail for attaching.

SPOTS

Make seven spots in Tropical Green and seven spots in Marmalade colour yarn.
Round 1: Make a MC with 8 dc (8 sts).
Fasten off round and leave a long tail for attaching.

ATTACHING PIECES AND ASSEMBLY

EYES AND CHEEKS

Details on how to outline the safety eyes in crochet thread can be found in the Finishing Touches section (see page 22).

Using the Bubblegum colour yarn, whip stitch or embroider a double line beginning on the round below the safety eyes, starting near the end of the safety eye and 3 stitches wide. Enter your thread through the bottom of the head and embroider the cheeks. Once finished, bring the needle back down through the head to where it entered. Knot the thread ends together and hide them within the head.

UNDERBELLY

Using pins, secure the underbelly to the front of Nessie with the first rows underneath the head at the start of the neck. Add more pins along the sides, making sure the underbelly is aligned with the nose and ends at round 66–67 of the tail. Adjust the piece to ensure that it is even on both sides and in the middle of the body. Once the piece is centred, use an embroidery needle and the extra yarn tail to sew the underbelly in place using mattress stitch.

FINS

Pin the front fins, with the decreases facing the neck, beginning at round 30 of the side of the body 1 stitch away from the underbelly piece. Then, angling the fin up towards the back, pin it between rounds 35 and 36, with 4–5 stitches between the back of the fin and the underbelly piece. Make sure Nessie is sitting up; if not, angle the fins towards the front of the body instead. Then whip stitch them in place with an embroidery needle and the yarn tails. Weave in and hide the leftover tail inside the body.

The back fins will be flipped opposite, with the decreases facing the tail. Pin starting between rounds 47 and 48 next to the underbelly piece and ending between rounds 50 and 51. There should be about 5 stitches separating the back of the fin and the underbelly piece, angled up towards the back like the front fins. Once both fins are pinned, whip stitch with an embroidery needle and the extra yarn tails. After both the back fins are sewn in place, weave in the extra yarn ends.

SPOTS

Pin the spots in clusters on the head, neck and body. Use an embroidery needle and the long yarn tail to secure each spot down in the pinned location with 2 mattress stitches (see page 21) opposite each other. Exit the needle through the head, body or neck and out.

Tie the two yarn ends together underneath each spot and weave them inside Nessie. Repeat the step for the 13 spots remaining (or more).

NESSIE THE LOCH NESS MONSTER

BANSHEE

The Banshee is a female spirit and messenger of death in Gaelic folklore whose appearance or wailing warned a family that one of them would die soon. She would be dressed in a flowing robe with long, wispy hair, floating through the night air, crying and shrieking.

Skill Level

Finished size

8in (20cm)

Supplies and materials

Universal Yarn Brand Bamboo Pop DK, 50% cotton, 50% bamboo (292yd/266m per 3½oz/100g):
Lily Pad 121, Blue Whisper 134, Cream 102, Silken 115, Graphite 120, Bubblegum 141

Crochet thread 10:
Black

Hook size: 2mm

Safety eyes: ½in (12mm)

Polyester fibre filling

Embroidery needles

Sewing pins

Stitch markers

Scissors

Pipe cleaners

BANSHEE

ARMS

Make two arms in Lily Pad colour yarn.
Work all the stitches in a round from bottom to top.
Do not stuff.
Wire will be added to the arms later.

Round 1: Make a MC with 6 dc (6 sts).
Round 2: (Dc2inc) 6 times (12 sts).
Rounds 3–6: Dc in each st around (12 sts).
Round 7: Dc 4, (dc2tog) twice, dc 4 (10 sts).
Rounds 8–19: Dc in each st around (10 sts).
Fasten off and hide tails inside the arms.

. . . .

ONE PIECE BODY AND HEAD

Start by making two legs in Lily Pad colour yarn.
Work all stitches in a round from bottom to top.
Stuff as you crochet.

Round 1: Make a MC with 9 dc (9 sts).
Round 2: (Dc2inc) 9 times (18 sts).
Round 3: Dc2inc, dc 6, (dc2inc) 4 times, dc 6, dc2inc (24 sts).
Rounds 4–6: Dc in each st around (24 sts).
Round 7: Dc 8, (dc2tog, dc) twice, dc2tog, dc 8 (21 sts).
Round 8: Dc 8, dc2tog, dc, dc2tog, dc 6, dc2tog (18 sts).
Round 9: Dc 7, (dc2tog) twice, dc 6, dc2inc (17 sts).
Round 10: Dc 8, dc2inc, dc 8 (18 sts).
Rounds 11–13: Dc in each st around (18 sts).
In the next two rounds, if the increases are not facing the front of the foot and the decreases at the back of the foot, adjust your starting dc stitch count by adding or subtracting 1–2 stitches.
Round 14: Dc 2, dc2tog, dc 5, (dc2inc) twice, dc 5, dc2tog (18 sts).
Round 15: Dc 8, dc2inc, dc 7, dc2tog (18 sts).
Round 16: Dc in each st around (18 sts).
Rounds 17–18: Dc 8, htr 6, dc 4 (18 sts).
Round 19: (Dc2inc) 3 times, dc 5, (dc2tog) 3 times, dc 4 (18 sts).
Rounds 20–21: Dc in each st around (18 sts).
Round 22: Sl st 6, dc 12 (18 sts).
Round 23: FLO sl st 6, dc 12 in both loops (18 sts).
Round 24: FLO dc 6, dc 12 in both loops (18 sts).
Please note: If you are on the first leg, cut the yarn and fasten off. If you are on the second leg, continue to Round 25. Not everyone's tension is the same. When you connect the legs, if they are not facing perfectly front, adjust your starting dc stitch count by adding or subtracting 1–2 stitches before chaining them together.
The chain in the next round counts as a stitch.
Round 25: Dc 10 (this will move the starting stitch to the other side of the leg to ensure both legs are facing forward), ch, dc to the first leg (make sure to connect the dc 1 stitch before where you fastened off), dc 17, dc in the back of the ch, dc 18 around 2nd leg (38 sts).
The ch between the back of the legs will be the new starting stitch.
Round 26: Dc in each st around (38 sts).
Please note: If there is a hole visible where the 2 legs are joined, use an embroidery needle and the leftover yarn from attaching the legs together to sew it closed with a whip stitch (see page 21).
Round 27: Dc 9, (dc2inc) twice, dc 17, (dc2inc) twice, dc 8 (42 sts).
Rounds 28–30: Dc in each st around (42 sts).
Round 31: Dc 9, (dc2tog) twice, dc 17, (dc2tog) twice, dc 8 (38 sts).
Rounds 32–33: Dc in each st around (38 sts).
Round 34: Dc 9, dc2tog, dc 17, dc2tog, dc 8 (36 sts).
Round 35: (Dc 2, dc2tog, dc 2) 6 times (30 sts).
Rounds 36–43: Dc in each st around (30 sts).

At this point, you will begin to add the arms. Remember that not everyone's tension is the same. When you add the left and right arms, if they are not parallel with the sides of the legs, add or subtract 1–2 stitches before their placement. Then adjust the starting point of the stitch marker to accommodate the extra stitches.

Round 44: Dc 7, dc 5 (place the first arm at the side of the body and stitch the body and arm together with the next 5 stitches. The hook will go through both the arm and the body, leaving the outside 5 stitches of the arm alone. Make sure the decreases from round 7 on the arms are facing forward), dc 10, dc 5 (place the second arm at the side of the body and stitch the body and arm together with the next 5 stitches, leaving the outside 5 stitches of the arm alone. Make sure the decreases from round 7 on the arms are facing forward), dc 3 (30 sts).
Round 45: Dc 7, dc 5 (stitching the 5 stitches along the outside of the arm), dc 10, dc 5 (stitching along the outside of the arm), dc 3 (30 sts).
Round 46: Dc in each st around (30 sts).

BANSHEE

Take two pipe cleaners and twist them together to make one thick pipe cleaner. Take the two ends and twist them together to make a point. Bring the bottom centre of the pipe cleaners up to the twist. This will create two long wires that you will feed down through both of the arms. Push the wire down in the first arm and then into the second arm. This will leave the ends of the wire coming up out of the neck.

Round 47: (Dc 3, dc2tog) 6 times (24 sts).
Round 48: (Dc, dc2tog, dc) 6 times (18 sts).
Round 49: (Dc 2, dc2tog, dc 2) 3 times (15 sts).
Round 50: Dc in each st around (15 sts).
Do not cut the yarn and continue to round 51 to make the head.

. . . .

HEAD

Round 51: FLO (dc 2, dc2inc, dc 2) 3 times (18 sts).
Round 52: FLO (dc, dc2inc, dc) 6 times (24 sts).
Round 53: FLO (dc 3, dc2inc) 6 times (30 sts).
Round 54: (Dc 2, dc2inc, dc 2) 6 times (36 sts).
Round 55: (Dc 5, dc2inc) 6 times (42 sts).
Round 56: (Dc 3, dc2inc, dc 3) 6 times (48 sts).
Round 57: (Dc 7, dc2inc) 6 times (54 sts).
Round 58: (Dc 4, dc2inc, dc 4) 6 times (60 sts).
Rounds 59–62: Dc in each st around (60 sts).
Round 63: Dc 30, ch, sk, dc 12, ch, sk, dc 16 (60 sts).
Please note: The chain spaces with the skip in round 63 will be where you place the safety eyes later in the pattern. The chain spaces should line up with the armpits of the doll. If they do not, adjust them left or right by a few stitches to get the correct placement, remembering to have 12 dc between each chain space.
Rounds 64–66: Dc in each st around (60 sts).
Round 67: (Dc 4, dc2tog, dc 4) 6 times (54 sts).
At this time, add the safety eyes in the chain spaces on round 63.

Round 68: (Dc 7, dc2tog) 6 times (48 sts).
Round 69: Dc in each st around (48 sts).
Round 70: (Dc 3, dc2tog, dc 3) 6 times (42 sts).
Round 71: (Dc 5, dc2tog) 6 times (36 sts).
Round 72: (Dc 2, dc2tog, dc 2) 6 times (30 sts).
Round 73: (Dc 3, dc2tog) 6 times (24 sts).
Round 74: (Dc, dc2tog, dc) 6 times (18 sts).
Round 75: (Dc, dc2tog) 6 times (12 sts).
Round 76: (Dc, dc2tog) 4 times (8 sts).
Fasten off and weave the yarn under each of the FLO, pull tight, and hide the end inside the head.

EARS

Make two ears in Lily Pad colour yarn.
Work all the stitches in a round.
Round 1: Make a MC with 9 dc (9 sts).
Fasten off and do not close the MC; leave it open with long tails to attach to the head.

HAIR

Work in rounds until instructed to work in chains.
First set of hair is worked in Blue Whisper colour yarn until instructed to change to Cream colour yarn.
Round 1: Make a MC with 6 dc (6 sts).
Round 2: (Dc2inc) 6 times (12 sts).
Round 3: (Dc, dc2inc) 6 times (18 sts).
Round 4: (Dc, dc2inc, dc) 6 times (24 sts).
Work the next rows in chains to create the hair strands. When crocheting in a chain, after turning, work the first dc stitch in the second chain from the hook. Then sl st to the next stitch in round 4 before starting the next row.
Rows 1–13: Ch 56, turn, dc 55 up the ch, sl st (55 sts) (13 rows of hair strands).
After row 13, sl st a colour change to Cream to the next st in round 4 before starting row 14.
Rows 14–24: Ch 56, turn, dc 55 up the ch, sl st (55 sts) (11 rows of hair strands).
Fasten off and leave a long tail for sewing.
Second set of hair is worked in Cream yarn.
Round 1: Make a MC with 6 dc (6 sts).
Round 2: (Dc2inc) 6 times (12 sts).
Round 3: (Dc, dc2inc) 6 times (18 sts).
Work the next rows in chains to create the hair strands. Remember, after turning, work the first dc stitch in the second chain from the hook. Then sl st to the next stitch in round 3 before starting the next row.
Rows 1–18: Ch 56, turn, dc 55 up the ch, sl st (55 sts) (18 rows of hair strands).
Fasten off and leave a long tail for sewing.

DRESS
TOP
Work in flat rows using Silken colour.
After each row, ch and turn and work back the other way.
Row 1: Ch 37, turn (37 sts).
Rows 2-5: Dc 36, ch, turn (36 sts).
Row 6: Dc 6, ch 9 (skipping 6 sts), dc 12, ch 9 (skipping 6 sts), dc 6, ch, turn (42 sts).
Row 7: Dc 16, dc2tog, dc 6, dc2tog, dc 16, ch, turn (40 sts).
Row 8: Dc 16, dc2tog, dc 4, dc2tog, dc 16, ch, turn (38 sts).
Row 9: Dc 17, (dc2tog) twice, dc 17 (36 sts).
Fasten off and weave in the end tails.

Round 9: Htr2inc, tr 2, tr2inc, tr 2, htr2inc, htr 2, dc 7, htr (20 sts).
Round 10: Htr, tr 4, tr2inc, tr2tog, tr2inc, tr 4, htr, dc 5, htr (21 sts).
Round 11: Htr, tr 5, tr2inc, tr, tr2inc, tr 5, htr, dc 5, htr (23 sts).
Round 12: Htr, (tr 2, tr2inc) twice, tr, dtr, (dtr, ch 3, turn and dc in the 3rd ch from hook, dtr) in the same st, dtr, tr, (tr2inc, tr 2) twice, htr 5 (31 sts).
Fasten off and weave in the end tails.
Repeat steps for the second sleeve. Make sure to begin in the bottom right-hand corner of the armhole so the longer stitches stay on the bottom of the second sleeve.

LONG SLEEVES
Work all stitches in a round from bottom to top.
Attach the Silken colour yarn to the bottom corner of the open armhole of the dress. Remember that there are 6 sts on the bottom and 9 sts on the top.
Round 1: FLO dc in the bottom right corner of the armhole that is before the first stitch, FLO dc 6, dc in the left bottom corner of the armhole, dc 9 on the upper armhole (17 sts).
Rounds 2-5: FLO dc 8, dc 9 (17 sts).
Rounds 6-7: FLO htr 8, dc 9 (17 sts).
Round 8: Htr, tr 7, htr, dc 7, htr (17 sts).

SKIRT

Turn dress top upside down with the front of the dress facing you, and attach the Silken colour yarn to the right corner of the dress with the first stitch.

Round 1: Dc 36, ch 2 (38 sts).

With the next round, the two sides will connect to crochet the skirt in rounds. Attach the first dc stitch of round 2 to the first stitch of round 1, then continue with the rest of the stitches in round 2.

Round 2: Dc, htr 5, htr2inc, htr 8, htr2inc, htr 4, (htr2inc, htr 8) twice (42 sts).
Round 3: (Htr 3, htr2inc, htr 3) 6 times (48 sts).
Round 4: Htr 34, (htr2inc, htr) twice, htr2inc, htr 9 (51 sts).
Round 5: Htr in each st around (51 sts).
Round 6: Htr 37, (htr2inc, htr) twice, htr2inc, htr 9 (54 sts).
Round 7: Htr in each st around (54 sts).
Round 8: Htr 40, (htr2inc, htr) twice, htr2inc, htr 9 (57 sts).
Round 9: Htr in each st around (57 sts).
Round 10: Htr 43, (htr2inc, htr) twice, htr2inc, htr 9 (60 sts).
Round 11: Htr in each st around (60 sts).
Round 12: Htr 46, (htr2inc, htr) twice, htr2inc, htr 9 (63 sts).
Round 13: Htr in each st around (63 sts).
Round 14: Htr 49, (htr2inc, htr) twice, htr2inc, htr 9 (66 sts).
Round 15: Htr in each st around (66 sts).
Round 16: Htr 52, (htr2inc, htr) twice, htr2inc, htr 9 (69 sts).
Round 17: Htr in each st around (69 sts).
Round 18: Htr 55, (htr2inc, htr) twice, htr2inc, htr 9 (72 sts).
Round 19: Htr in each st around (72 sts).

The next round will have chain loops. After the three chains, the next dc will be in the same stitch as the last dc. This will make the loop. Make sure to do this after each set of three chains.

Round 20: Dc 2, ch 3, dc in the same st as the last dc, dc 2, (ch 3, dc 7, ch 3, dc 5, ch 3, dc 3) 5 times, ch 3, dc 9 (140 sts).
Fasten off and weave in the end tails.

ROPE

Work all stitches in a chain using Graphite yarn colour.
Row 1: Ch 160 (160 sts).
Fasten off and leave a long tail.

BANSHEE

ATTACHING PIECES AND ASSEMBLY

EYES

Using black crochet thread, push the needle through the bottom of the head and out at the inside bottom corner of the first eye (I tend to use a smaller embroidery needle with a sharp tip for this). Then insert your needle back through the top outside corner of the eye (diagonal corner of the eye). Pull the thread through the head and out the same stitch or near where you entered. This adds a stripe to the lower portion of the eye. Do not pull too tight otherwise the thread may slip under the eye.

To make the black streaking on the lower part of the eye, bring the needle back up through the top outside corner of the safety eye and then back down for two and a half rounds. This adds the first streak. To finish the two to four streaks, bring the needle back up to the bottom of the safety eye and add the streaks a little bit apart and at different lengths. Once all the streaks are finished, take the needle back through the bottom of the head at the starting point, tie it off, and hide the thread tails inside the head. Then repeat the steps for the second eye.

These next steps will mimic the first ones, but now you will outline the top of the eye. With black crochet thread, push the needle through the bottom of the head and out, at the inside bottom corner of the first eye. Insert your needle back through the top outside corner of the eye (diagonal corner of the eye), but a stitch away from the bottom, back outlining thread. Pull the thread through the head and out the same stitch or near where you entered. This will add a stripe on the upper portion of the eye. Do not pull too tight otherwise the thread may slip under the eye. Secure this thread in place by having it come back up and circle the middle of the thread strand. Take the needle back through the bottom of the head at the starting point, tie it off and hide the thread tail inside the head. Then repeat the steps for the second eye.

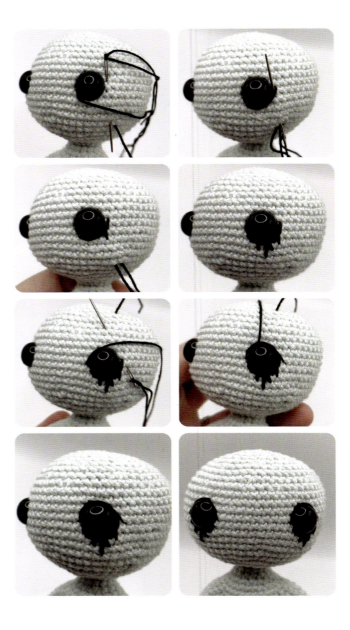

100 CROCHETED MYTHICAL CREATURES

NOSE AND CHEEKS

Using pins, mark the width of the nose in the centre of the face between rounds 61 and 62 and 3 stitches apart.
Use Lily Pad colour yarn. With an embroidery needle, enter the yarn through the side of the head to the first nose pin. Whip stitch (see page 21) a nose at the two pins four or five times. Exit the yarn back through the same stitch on the side of the head, knot the two ends, and weave the ends into the head.

Using the Bubblegum coloured yarn, whip stitch or embroider a double line beginning on the round below the safety eyes, starting near the end of the safety eye and 3 stitches wide. Enter your thread through the bottom of the head and embroider the cheeks. Once finished, bring the needle back down through the head where it entered. Knot the thread ends together and hide them within its head. Repeat the steps for the second cheek.

EARS

Pin the ears on the side of the head between rounds 62 and 64 with 7 stitches between the bottom of the ears and the side of the safety eye. When pinned evenly, whip stitch them on using an embroidery needle and the leftover yarn ends. Weave the extra tails into the head.

BANSHEE

ATTACHING THE HAIR

Match up the MC of the first larger hairpiece and the MC of the head and add a pin to the top of the hair to keep it in place. The Cream colour hair strands should be facing the front of the head. Pin the 13 Blue Whisper hair strands to the back of the head two rounds below the bottom of the ears, side by side to cover it. Adjust the hair strands as needed to fill any bare spots.

Sew the hair using an embroidery needle and the long Cream colour tail left over from making the hair. Starting at the top of the hair, make a few whip stitches around a few stitches on the outside rounds, making sure to go through both the hair and the head to keep the hair from moving around. Next, flip the head upside down and sew the hair strands down with the left-over Blue Whisper yarn tail, beginning at the pins along the back hair strands and working your way around the back of the head.

Next, match up the MC of the second smaller hairpiece and the MC of the first hairpiece and add a pin to the top of that hair to keep it in place. Then sew the smaller hairpiece on with the same steps as the first hairpiece. Make sure the embroidery needle goes through both hair pieces when whip stitching along the outside rounds. Sew three of the front Cream colour hair strands to the top of the forehead to keep the hair flipped back out of the face. If you wish to keep the hair behind the ears, whip stitch a few of the Cream colour hair strands in place as well. Once finished, hide all the left-over yarn tails inside the head.

DRESS

Pull the dress up and over the feet onto the body, then push the arms through both of the sleeves. Flip the doll over and sew the back of the dress closed with mattress stitch (see page 21) using an embroidery needle and the Silken colour yarn. This will close the opening of the dress and give a smooth seam. Weave in the loose yarn tails to finish off.

Wrap the rope around the waist of the dress three times. Then tie a lower knot with the ends leaving two long chains. Trim any extra yarn ends that are too long.

CHERRY BLOSSOM DRYAD

Tree nymphs, also known as dryads, are beautiful, shy, female spirits that live within the trees of enchanted forests, glens and sacred wooded areas. When the tree changes for the season, the dryad changes, and if the tree dies, the spirit will die with it because the two are forever linked.

Skill Level

Finished size

7½in (19cm)

Supplies and materials

Universal Yarn Brand Bamboo Pop DK, 50% cotton, 50% bamboo (292yd/266m per 3½oz/100g): Hickory 151, Apricot Slush 135, Super Pink 114, Almond 148, Lime Green 108, Bubblegum 141

Crochet thread 10:
Black, white, brown

Hook size: 2mm

Safety eyes: ½in (12mm)

Polyester fibre filling

Embroidery needles

Sewing pins

Stitch markers

Scissors

Small clear plastic hairbands or ties

Pipe cleaners

ARMS

Make two arms in Hickory colour yarn.
Work all the stitches in a round from bottom to top.
Do not stuff.
Wire will be added to the arms later.

Round 1: Make a MC with 6 dc (6 sts).
Round 2: (Dc2inc) 6 times (12 sts).
Rounds 3-6: Dc in each st around (12 sts).
Round 7: Dc 4, (dc2tog) twice, dc 4 (10 sts).
Rounds 8-20: Dc in each st around (10 sts).
Fasten off and hide the leftover tails inside the arms.

ONE PIECE BODY AND HEAD

Start by making two legs in Hickory colour.
Work all stitches in a round from bottom to top.
Stuff as you crochet.

Round 1: Make a MC with 9 dc (9 sts).
Round 2: (Dc2inc) 9 times (18 sts).
Round 3: Dc2inc, dc 6, (dc2inc) 4 times, dc 6, dc2inc (24 sts).
Round 4: FLO sl st 10, dc, htr, ch 2, htr, dc, sl st 10 (24 sts).
Fasten off and weave tails inside the rounds.
Attach Hickory colour yarn to the BLO of round 3 on the back side of the leg. This will give a cleaner look to the stitch change.
Round 5: BLO dc in each st around (24 sts).
Round 6: Dc in each st around (24 sts).
Round 7: Dc 8, (dc2tog, dc) twice, dc2tog, dc 8 (21 sts).
Round 8: Dc 8, dc2tog, dc, dc2tog, dc 6, dc2tog (18 sts).
Rounds 9-20: Dc in each st around (18 sts).
Please note: If you are on the first leg, cut the yarn and fasten off. If you are on the second leg, continue to Round 21. Not everyone's tension is the same. When you connect the legs, if they are not facing perfectly front, adjust your starting dc stitch count by adding or subtracting 1–2 stitches before chaining them together.

The chain in the next round counts as a stitch.
Round 21: Dc 6 (this will move the starting stitch to the side of the leg to ensure the legs are facing slightly towards the outside), ch, dc to the 1st leg (where you fasten off), dc 17, dc in the back of the connecting ch, dc 18 around 2nd leg (38 sts). The chain between the back of the legs will be the new starting stitch.
Round 22: Dc in each st around (38 sts).
Please note: If there is a hole visible where the two legs are joined, use an embroidery needle and a short length of yarn to sew it closed with a whip stitch.
Round 23: Dc 9, (dc2inc) twice, dc 17, (dc2inc) twice, dc 8 (42 sts).
Rounds 24-26: Dc in each st around (42 sts).
Round 27: Dc 9, (dc2tog) twice, dc 17, (dc2tog) twice, dc 8 (38 sts).
Rounds 28-29: Dc in each st around (38 sts).
Round 30: Dc 9, dc2tog, dc 17, dc2tog, dc 8 (36 sts).
Round 31: (Dc 2, dc2tog, dc 2) 6 times (30 sts).
Rounds 32-39: Dc in each st around (30 sts).
At this point, you will begin to add the arms. Remember that not everyone's tension is the same. When you add the left and right arms, if they are not parallel with the sides of the legs, add or subtract 1–2 stitches before their placement.

Then adjust the starting point of the stitch marker to accommodate the extra stitches.

Round 40: Dc 7, dc 5 (place the first arm at the side of the body and stitch the body and arm together with the next 5 stitches. The hook will go through both the arm and the body, leaving the outside 5 stitches of the arm alone. Make sure the decreases from round 7 on the arms are facing forward), dc 10, dc 5 (place the second arm at the side of the body and stitch the body and arm together with the next 5 stitches, leaving the outside 5 stitches of the arm alone. Make sure the decreases from round 7 on the arms are facing forward), dc 3 (30 sts).

Round 41: Dc 7, dc 5 (stitching the 5 stitches along the outside of the arm), dc 10, dc 5 (stitching the 5 stitches along the outside of the arm), dc 3 (30 sts).

Round 42: Dc in each st around (30 sts).

Fasten off and hide the tails inside the body.

Take two pipe cleaners and twist them together to make one thick pipe cleaner. Take the two ends and twist them together to make a point. Bring the bottom centre of the pipe cleaners up to the twist. This will create two long wires that you will feed down through both of the arms. Push the wire down in the first arm and then into the second arm. This will leave the ends of the wire coming up out of the top of the body.

Attach Apricot Slush colour yarn to round 42 at the fasten-off.

Round 43: (Dc 3, dc2tog) 6 times (24 sts).

Round 44: (Dc, dc2tog, dc) 6 times (18 sts).

Round 45: (Dc 2, dc2tog, dc 2) 3 times (15 sts).

Round 46: Dc in each st around (15 sts).

Do not cut the yarn and continue to round 47 to make the head.

CHERRY BLOSSOM DRYAD

HEAD

Round 47: FLO (dc 2, dc2inc, dc 2) 3 times (18 sts).
Round 48: FLO (dc, dc2inc, dc) 6 times (24 sts).
Round 49: FLO (dc 3, dc2inc) 6 times (30 sts).
Round 50: (Dc 2, dc2inc, dc 2) 6 times (36 sts).
Round 51: (Dc 5, dc2inc) 6 times (42 sts).
Round 52: (Dc 3, dc2inc, dc 3) 6 times (48 sts).
Round 53: (Dc 7, dc2inc) 6 times (54 sts).
Round 54: (Dc 4, dc2inc, dc 4) 6 times (60 sts).
Rounds 55–58: Dc in each st around (60 sts).
Round 59: Dc 30, ch, sk, dc 12, ch, sk, dc 16 (60 sts).
Please note: The chain spaces with the skip in round 59 will be where you place the safety eyes later in the pattern. The chain spaces should line up with the armpits of the doll. If they do not, adjust them left or right by a few stitches to get the correct placement, remembering to have 12 dc between each chain space.
Rounds 60–62: Dc in each st around (60 sts).
Round 63: (Dc 4, dc2tog, dc 4) 6 times (54 sts).
At this time, add the safety eyes in the chain spaces on round 59.
Round 64: (Dc 7, dc2tog) 6 times (48 sts).
Round 65: Dc in each st around (48 sts).
Round 66: (Dc 3, dc2tog, dc 3) 6 times (42 sts).
Round 67: (Dc 5, dc2tog) 6 times (36 sts).
Round 68: (Dc 2, dc2tog, dc 2) 6 times (30 sts).
Round 69: (Dc 3, dc2tog) 6 times (24 sts).
Round 70: (Dc, dc2tog, dc) 6 times (18 sts).
Round 71: (Dc, dc2tog) 6 times (12 sts).
Round 72: (Dc, dc2tog) 4 times (8 sts).
Fasten off and weave the yarn under each of the FLO, pull tight, and hide the end inside the head.

EARS

Make two ears in Apricot Slush colour.
Work all the stitches in a round.
Round 1: Make a MC with dc 2, htr 2, tr, ch 3, turn, sl st in the 3rd ch from hook, tr, htr 2, dc 2 (13 sts).
Fasten off and do not close the MC; leave it open with long tails to attach to the head.

HAIR

Using Super Pink colour, work in rounds until instructed to work in chains.

Round 1: Make a MC with 6 dc (6 sts).
Round 2: (Dc2inc) 6 times (12 sts).
Round 3: (Dc, dc2inc) 6 times (18 sts).
Round 4: (Dc, dc2inc, dc) 6 times (24 sts).
Round 5: (Dc 3, dc2inc) 6 times (30 sts).

Work the next rows in chains to create the hair strands. When crocheting in a chain, after turning, work the first dc stitch in the second chain from the hook. Then sl st to the next stitch in round 5 before starting the next row.

Rows 1–18: Ch 56, turn, dc 55 up the ch (55 sts) (18 rows of hair strands sts).
Rows 19–30: Ch 36, turn, dc 35 up the ch (35 sts) (12 rows of hair strands sts).
Fasten off and leave a long tail for sewing.

CHEST PIECE

Work in flat rows using Hickory colour.
When turning, always dc in the second stitch or chain from the hook, working back the other way.

Row 1: Ch 38, turn (38 sts).
Row 2: Dc 6, (htr, tr, ch 3, turn, sl st in the 3rd ch from hook, tr, htr in the same stitch), dc 4, (htr, ch 3, turn, sl st in the 3rd ch from hook, htr in the same stitch), dc 3, (htr, ch 3, turn, sl st in the 3rd ch from hook, htr in the same stitch), dc 2, (htr, tr, ch 3, turn, sl st in the 3rd ch from hook, tr, htr in the same stitch), dc 2, (htr, ch 3, turn, sl st in the 3rd ch from hook, htr in the same stitch), dc 3, (htr, ch 3, turn, sl st in the 3rd ch from hook, htr in the same stitch), dc 4, (htr, tr, ch 3, turn, sl st in the 3rd ch from hook, tr, htr in the same stitch), dc 6 (71 sts).

Fasten off and leave a long tail for attaching.

BODY SWIRLS

Using Almond colour, make two swirls.
Row 1: Ch 35 (35 sts).
Fasten off and leave a long tail for attaching.

CHERRY BLOSSOM DRYAD

LEAVES

Make ten leaves in Lime Green colour yarn. Work all the stitches in the magic circle.

Round 1: Make a MC with dc, htr, tr, ch 3, turn, sl st in the 3rd ch from hook, tr, htr, dc 2 (10 sts).

Fasten off and leave a long tail for attaching.

FLOWERS

Make 15–16 flowers in Bubblegum colour yarn. Work all the stitches in the magic circle.

Round 1: Make a MC with dc, (tr 2, sl st) 5 times (16 sts).

Fasten off and leave a long tail for attaching.

ATTACHING PIECES AND ASSEMBLY

EYES

Details on how to outline the safety eyes in crochet thread can be found in the Finishing Touches section (see page 22).

NOSE AND CHEEKS

Using pins, mark the width of the nose in the centre of the face between rounds 56 and 57 and 3 stitches apart. Using Apricot Slush yarn. With a small embroidery needle, enter the yarn through the side of the head to the first nose pin. Whip stitch (see page 21) a nose at the two pins 4–5 times. Exit the yarn back through the same stitch on the side of the head, knot the two ends, and weave the ends into the head.

Using the Bubblegum colour yarn, whip stitch or embroider a double line beginning on the round below the safety eyes, starting near the end of the safety eye and 3 stitches wide. Enter your thread through the bottom of the head and embroider the cheeks. Once finished, bring the needle back down through the head to where it entered. Knot the thread ends together and hide them within its head.

EARS

Pin the ears on the side of the head between rounds 57 and 58 with 7 stitches between the bottom opening of the ears and the safety eyes. Make sure that the two ears are pointing slightly upwards. If not, flip the one opposite ear over to get the same look as the other ear.

When pinned evenly on both sides of the head, use an embroidery needle to sew on using the leftover yarn ends. Weave the extra tails into the head.

CHEST PIECE

Pin the chest piece around the back of the neck at the colour change and pin the longest point to round 29. With the pins in place, flip the chest piece up and start sewing it to the body using mattress stitch (see page 21) and an embroidery needle. The first stitch will go through a stitch on the body; then bring the embroidery needle up through the stitch on the chest piece. Make sure to keep the chest piece in the same spot and pinned when sewing around the whole piece. Once complete, weave in and hide the leftover tails inside the body.

CHERRY BLOSSOM DRYAD

ATTACHING THE HAIR

Match up the MC of the hair piece and the MC of the head and add a pin to the top of the hair to keep it in place. Pin 16 of the hair strands to the back of the head, behind the ears and side by side. Adjust the hair strands as needed to fill any bare spots. Pin the last two longer hair strands in front of the ears. Leave the shorter hair strand loose until after the long hair is in place and sewn onto the head.

Sew the hair using an embroidery needle and the long tail left over from making the hair. Starting at the top of the hair, make a few whip stitches around a few of the stitches on the outside rounds. Make sure to go through both the hair and the head to keep the hair from moving around. Next, flip the head upside down and sew the hair strands down with a whip stitch, beginning at the pins along the back hair strands and working your way around the back of the head.

Using two small, clear hairbands or ties, make ponytails behind each of the ears. First split the back 16 hair strands in half with a parting in the centre. Pull eight hair strands up to one side just above the ear. Then, at the front of the face, skip the first two loose hair strands near the ear, and grab the next three shorter hair strands. Add them to the eight from the back of the head. Wrap the hairband around the gathered hair strands to create a high ponytail. Repeat the steps for the second ponytail.

Working at the front of the head, there should be four shorter hair strands left. Take the two outside shorter pieces and pin them back to drape behind the ears. Once in place, sew on with an embroidery needle and the leftover yarn. Weave the end of the yarn in the hair and head to finish off. Take the last two hair strands in front of the face and lay them over to the right out of the way. Remove any pins that have not been removed already.

112 CROCHETED MYTHICAL CREATURES

ATTACHING SMALL SWIRLS AND LEAVES

Pin the two chains in swirl shapes onto the front of the legs and body. Use lots of pins on each to get the shape and size of the swirls that you like. Then, using a sewing needle and brown sewing thread, sew each of the long pieces to the body with a whip stitch. To get a clean look to each of them, make sure the tops of the chains are facing up and they do not twist. When whip stitching, bring the needle up through the centre of the chain and then down through the body. This will attach the centre of the chain and make for a more even look for each of the swirls. Once finished, weave in the thread and hide the leftover yarn tails inside the body.

Before sewing the leaves, pin six of them in pairs on the right hip, left outer thigh and the top of the left arm. Save the last four leaves to sew to a few flowers on the head of the dryad. Using an embroidery needle and the extra yarn tails, sew the base of each of the leaves in their pinned places. Once complete, hide all the tails inside the body.

FLOWERS

The flowers can be sewn on the hair strands at any point on the head. The exact placement is your choice, but they should be evenly separated with eight flowers for the left and eight flowers for the right side of the hair. Use an embroidery needle and the leftover yarn tails to whip stitch each of the flowers to the hair. Once finished, tie the two yarn ends from each flower together tightly, then weave each end into the back of the flowers. Trim off any extra yarn to complete.

Take the remaining four leaves and sew them to the backs of four of the flowers, making sure to spread them out around the head for symmetry. Tie the ends together and weave each of the ends into the leaves. Trim the extra yarn to complete.

CHERRY BLOSSOM DRYAD

UNICORN

Unicorns have been popular mythical creatures for centuries. Their iconic single horn and majestic appearance have captured the imaginations of people worldwide. Powerful and untamable, the unicorn is often associated with purity, grace and magic, and possibly uses its healing powers to purify water with its horn. The magical nature of this creature adds to its appeal, with many people still searching for proof of their existence.

Skill Level

Finished size

8½in (22cm)

Supplies and materials

Universal Yarn Brand Bamboo Pop DK, 50% cotton, 50% bamboo (292yd/266m per 3½oz/100g): White 101, Silken 115, Graphite 120, Bubblegum 141

Crochet thread 10:
Black, white, silver

Hook size: 2mm

Safety eyes: 9/16in (14mm)

Polyester fibre filling

Embroidery needles

Scissors

Stitch markers

Sewing pins

THE UNICORN

HEAD AND NECK

Using White colour yarn, work all stitches in a round from top to bottom. Stuff as you crochet.

Round 1: Make a MC with 6 dc (6 sts).
Round 2: (Dc2inc) 6 times (12 sts).
Round 3: (Dc, dc2inc) 6 times (18 sts).
Round 4: (Dc, dc2inc, dc) 6 times (24 sts).
Round 5: (Dc 3, dc2inc) 6 times (30 sts).
Round 6: (Dc 2, dc2inc, dc 2) 6 times (36 sts).
Round 7: (Dc 5, dc2inc) 6 times (42 sts).
Round 8: (Dc 3, dc2inc, dc 3) 6 times (48 sts).
Round 9: (Dc 7, dc2inc) 6 times (54 sts).
Round 10: (Dc 4, dc2inc, dc 4) 6 times (60 sts).
Round 11: (Dc 9, dc2inc) 6 times (66 sts).
Round 12: (Dc 5, dc2inc, dc 5) 6 times (72 sts).
Round 13: Dc 48, leaving 24 dc sts unworked (48 sts). Place a stitch marker on the 2 unworked stitches, stitch 49 and stitch 72 of round 12. This will mark the neck section to work later in the pattern. The next set of rounds will create the head only, by working around the 48 stitches of round 13. Fold the piece in half and work round 14.
Round 14: Dc in each st around (48 sts).
Round 15: (Dc 7, dc2inc) 6 times (54 sts).
Round 16: Dc in each st around (54 sts).
Round 17: (Dc 7, dc2tog) 6 times (48 sts).
Round 18: Dc 16, ch, sk, dc 16, ch, sk, dc 14 (48 sts).
Please note: The chain spaces with the skip in round 18 will be where you place the safety eyes later in the pattern.
Round 19: Dc in each st around (48 sts).
Round 20: Dc 9, dc2tog, dc 10, (dc2tog, dc) twice, dc2tog, dc 10, dc2tog, dc 5, dc2tog (42 sts).
Round 21: Dc in each st around (42 sts).
Round 22: (Dc 5, dc2tog) 6 times (36 sts).

At this time, add the safety eyes in the chain spaces on round 18.

CROCHETED MYTHICAL CREATURES

Round 23: Dc in each st around (36 sts).
Round 24: Dc 17, (dc2tog) 3 times, dc 13 (33 sts).
Round 25: Dc 17, (dc2inc) 3 times, dc 13 (36 sts)
Round 26: (Dc 2, dc2tog, dc 2) 6 times (30 sts).
Round 27: Dc in each st around (30 sts).
At this point, if you haven't started to stuff the head, start the stuffing now.
Round 28: (Dc 3, dc2tog) 6 times (24 sts).
Round 29: (Dc, dc2tog, dc) 6 times (18 sts).
Round 30: (Dc, dc2tog) 6 times (12 sts).
Before the last round and fastening off, add more stuffing to the snout and pack it fairly tight to help keep the shape of the head.
Round 31: (Dc, dc2tog) 4 times (8 sts).
Fasten off and weave the yarn under each of the FLO, then pull tight. Bring an embroidery needle down through the centre of the magic circle and out the bottom of the head. Pull slightly to flatten round 31 and hide the end inside the head.
Attach the White colour yarn to the first stitch of the open neck from round 13 and work all stitches in a round from right to left.
Stuff as you crochet, making sure to stuff the bottom of the head and the opening of the top of the neck. The hole left over from connecting the two pieces will be closed when the body is finished.
Rounds 14-17: Dc in each st around (24 sts).
Round 18: (Dc 3, dc2inc) 6 times (30 sts).
Rounds 19-22: Dc in each st around (30 sts).
Round 23: Dc 17, leave the rest of the round unworked (17 sts).
Fasten off and leave a long tail for attaching.
There will be a hole visible where the head and neck connect; use an embroidery needle and the leftover yarn from starting round 14 to sew it closed with 3-4 whip stitches (see page 21). If the yarn end is lost inside the neck, cut a new long piece of White yarn.

FRONT LEGS

Start by making two hooves in Graphite colour yarn, then continue to make two full legs.
Work all stitches in a round from bottom to top.
Stuff as you crochet.

Round 1: Make a MC with 9 dc (9 sts).
Round 2: (Dc2inc) 9 times (18 sts).
Round 3: BLO dc in each st around (18 sts).
Rounds 4-5: Dc in each st around (18 sts).
Fasten off and weave tails inside the rounds.
The next section will instruct you to make two different front legs.

BENT LEG

Attach White colour yarn to the BLO of round 5.
Round 6: BLO dc in each st around (18 sts).
Rounds 7-14: Dc in each st around (18 sts).
Round 15: Dc 7, htr 6, dc 5 (18 sts).
Round 16: (Dc2inc) 3 times, dc 4, htr 6, dc 5 (21 sts).
Round 17: Dc 10, (dc2tog) 3 times, Dc 5 (18 sts).
Rounds 18-23: Dc in each st around (18 sts).
Fasten off and weave the yarn end into the legs.

Add a stitch marker 8 stitches to the left of the last stitch on round 23. This will mark the location where it will be attached to the underbody. This is for the knee of the bent leg to be forward.

STRAIGHT LEG

Attach White colour yarn to the BLO of round 5.

Round 6: BLO dc in each st around (18 sts).

Rounds 7-23: Dc in each st around (18 sts).

Fasten off and weave the yarn end into the legs.

Add a stitch marker to the last stitch. This will mark the location where it will be attached to the underbody.

BACK LEGS

Start by making 2 hooves in Graphite colour yarn, then continue to make 2 full legs. Work all stitches in a round from bottom to top.

Stuff as you crochet.

Round 1: Make a MC with 9 dc (9 sts).

Round 2: (Dc2inc) 9 times (18 sts).

Round 3: BLO dc in each st around (18 sts).

Rounds 4-5: Dc in each st around (18 sts).

Fasten off and weave tails inside the rounds.

Attach White colour yarn to the BLO of round 5.

Round 6: BLO dc in each st around (18 sts).

Rounds 7-13: Dc in each st around (18 sts).

Rounds 14-15: Dc 7, htr 6, dc 5 (18 sts).

Round 16: (Dc2inc) 3 times, dc 4, (dc2tog) 3 times, dc 5 (18 sts).

Rounds 17-19: Dc in each st around (18 sts).

Round 20: (Dc, dc2inc) 3 times, dc 4, (dc2inc, dc) twice, dc2inc, dc 3 (24 sts).

Rounds 21-24: Dc in each st around (24 sts).

Fasten off and weave the yarn end into the legs.

Add a stitch marker to the first back leg, on the 1st st of the last round. This will mark the location where it will be attached to the underbody.

Add a stitch marker to the second back leg, on the 12th st of the last round. This will mark the location where it will be attached to the underbody. It is helpful to use different colours to ensure you are putting the correct leg on the correct side.

BODY

Using White colour yarn, work all the stitches in a round after row 1, from top to bottom.

The first section is the making of the underbody. Then you will connect each of the legs before moving

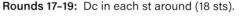

on to the construction of the main body portion.

After each row, turn and work back the other way, placing the first dc in the second st from the hook.

Row 1: Ch 12, turn (12 sts).

Round 2: Dc 10, dc 4 in the next st, dc 10, dc 4 in the next st (28 sts).

Round 3: Dc 10, (Dc2inc) 4 times, dc 10, (Dc2inc) 4 times (36 sts).

Round 4: Dc 12, (Dc2inc) 4 times, dc 14, (Dc2inc) 4 times, dc (44 sts).

The next round, connect each of the legs in the order in which they are listed. Make sure the hook goes under both loops on the inside of the leg and both loops on the inside of the underbody stitch when connecting.

Before connecting the first leg, flip the underbody over so the inside stitches (wrong side) face upwards. This way the

correct side will be on the outside of the unicorn and the continuing crochet stitches will match.

Round 5: Dc 11, dc 4 (connect the first back leg to the underbody with these dc sts, starting with the location of the stitch marker. The first leg will have the stitch marker next to the underbody and the knee of the leg facing away from the body), dc 4 along the back curve of the underbody, dc 4 (connect the second back leg to the underbody with these dc sts, starting with the location of the stitch marker. Both back legs should have the knees at the end of the underbody matching up and not below), dc 11 along the third side of the underbody, dc 4 (connect the straight front leg to the underbody with 4 dc sts, starting with the location of the stitch marker), dc 2 along the front curve of the underbody, dc 4 (connect the bent front leg to the underbody with these dc sts, starting with the location of the stitch marker. The knees should be facing forward at the end of the underbody), dc 11 along the first side of the underbody (this will move your starting st) (54 sts).

The next round will crochet the body around the underbody and the outsides of the four legs.

Round 6: Dc in the 1st st on the back leg, dc 19 around the leg, dc 4 on the back curve of the underbody, dc 20 around the 2nd back leg, dc 11 on the side of the underbody, dc 14 on the straight front leg, dc 2 on the front curve of the underbody, dc 14 on the bent front leg, dc 11 on the side of the underbody (96 sts).

Rounds 7–8: Dc in each st around (96 sts).

The two increases in the next round need to be in the 2 dc stiches between the front legs. If they are not, adjust the first dc stitches in the round by adding or subtracting 1–2 stitches.

Round 9: Dc 69, (dc2inc) twice, dc 25 (98 sts).

The last decrease on the next round will overlap onto the first stitch, making the end stitch count in the round 1 extra stitch.

Round 10: Dc 21, dc2tog, dc 20, dc2tog, dc 9, dc2tog, dc 30, dc2tog, dc 9, dc2tog (94 sts).

Round 11: Dc 19, dc2tog, dc 20, dc2tog, dc 7, dc2tog, dc 30, dc2tog, dc 7, dc2tog (88 sts).

Round 12: Dc 19, dc2tog, dc 19, dc2tog, dc 5, dc2tog, dc 30, dc2tog, dc 5, dc2tog (83 sts).

Round 13: Dc 19, dc2tog, dc 18, dc2tog, dc 3, dc2tog, dc 30, dc2tog, dc 3, dc2tog (78 sts).

Round 14: Dc 19, dc2tog, dc 17, dc2tog, dc, dc2tog, dc 30, dc2tog, dc, dc2tog (73 sts).
Round 15: (Dc, dc2tog) 4 times, dc 6, dc2tog, dc 6, (dc2tog, dc) 3 times, dc2tog, dc 36 (64 sts).
Round 16: Dc in each st around (64 sts).
Round 17: Dc 6, (dc2tog, dc) twice, dc2tog, dc 3, dc2tog, (dc, dc2tog) twice, dc 39 (58 sts).
Round 18: Dc in each st around (58 sts).
Round 19: Dc 6, dc2tog, dc, dc2tog, dc 2, dc2tog, dc, dc2tog, dc 40 (54 sts).
Round 20: Dc in each st around (54 sts).
Round 21: Dc 6, dc2tog, dc, (dc2tog) twice, dc, dc2tog, dc 38 (50 sts).
Round 22: Dc in each st around (50 sts).

Place two stitch markers in stitch 20 and stitch 49 of round 22, marking the starting and ending stitch to attach the neck and head later in the pattern.

Fasten off and hide the yarn end in the body.

At this time, finish stuffing the tops of all the legs, underbody and the unicorn's back.

Cut an extra-long piece of White yarn to sew the back closed. With an embroidery needle and the new piece of yarn, bring the needle up through the underbody and out the 10th stitch on the last round at the bottom of the curve. This should be the halfway point of the lower stitches. Make sure to leave a small tail to tie off later. Whip stitch (see page 21) the back closed, working in the FLO of each stitch directly across from each other and pulling the yarn tight after every 2 whip stitches. Bring the embroidery needle back through the underbody at the same location it entered.

If there is a small bump on the back near the start of the FLO whip stitches, add extra stuffing into that section and push it flat. If it is still there, bring the needle up through the bump and back down a stitch over, through the bottom of the underbody at the stitch it entered. Then pull slightly to flatten and tie the ends together. Push the knot through the stitch and into the body to hide it.

EARS

Make two ears using White colour yarn, working all the stitches in a round from top to bottom.
Do not stuff.
Round 1: Make a MC with 4 dc (4 sts).
Round 2: (Dc, dc2inc) twice (6 sts).
Round 3: (Dc2inc) 6 times (12 sts).
Round 4: (Dc, dc2inc) 6 times (18 sts).
Rounds 5–8: Dc in each st around (18 sts).
Do not close the ears. Fasten off and leave a long tail for attaching.

HORN

With the Silver crochet thread, work all the stitches in a round from bottom to top.
Stuff as you crochet.

Round 1: Make a MC with 12 dc (12 sts).
Do not pull the string to the magic circle tight.
Rounds 2–4: Dc in each st around (12 sts).
Round 5: (Dc 2, dc2tog, dc 2) twice (10 sts).
Rounds 6–8: Dc in each st around (10 sts).
Round 9: (Dc 3, dc2tog) twice (8 sts).
Rounds 10–12: Dc in each st around (8 sts).
Round 13: (Dc, dc2tog, dc) twice (6 sts).
Rounds 14–15: Dc in each st around (6 sts).
Round 16: (Dc, dc2tog) twice (4 sts).
Fasten off and weave the yarn under each of the FLO, pull tight and bring the thread down through the horn to use for sewing later.

HAIR

Using White colour yarn, work all the stitches in a flat row.
After each row, turn and work back the other way, placing the first dc in the second st from the hook.

Row 1: Ch 66, turn, dc in each st across (65 sts) (1 hair strand row).
Rows 2–16: Ch 66, turn, dc in each st across (65 sts) (15 rows of hair strands).

Twist each of the rows to create curls. Then fold the hair in half between rows 8 and 9 to pair up a portion of the curls.
Dc through both sides to create a top seam. There should be approximately 16 dc stitches along the top of the curls to create the seam (16 sts).
Fasten off and leave a long tail for attaching.

TAIL

Using White colour yarn, work all the stitches in a flat row.
After each row, turn and work back the other way, placing the first dc in the 2nd st from the hook.

Row 1: Ch 66, turn, dc in each st across (65 sts) (1 hair strand row).
Rows 2–8: Ch 66, turn, dc in each st across (65 sts) (7 rows of hair strands).

Twist each of the rows to create curls. Then fold the hair in half between rows 4 and 5 to pair up a portion of the curls.
Dc through both sides to create a top seam. There should be approximately 8 dc stitches along the top of the curls to create the seam. Fold the seam in half once more and dc 4 stitches along the top seam (4 sts).
Fasten off and leave a long tail for attaching.

UNICORN

ATTACHING PIECES AND ASSEMBLY

EYES AND CHEEKS

Details on how to outline the safety eyes in crochet thread can be found in the Finishing Touches section (see page 22).

Using the Bubblegum colour yarn, whip stitch or embroider a double line beginning about a round below the safety eyes, starting at the middle of the safety eye and 3 stitches wide. Enter an embroidery needle through the bottom of the head and Make two horizontal whip stitches where you marked the cheeks with the pins. Once finished, bring the needle back down through the head to where it entered. Knot the yarn ends together and hide them within the head.

NOSTRILS

Before whip stitching, follow the next steps to place pins marking both nostrils and ensuring they are even with the safety eyes. Mark the nostrils 6 rounds down from the safety eyes, 2 stitches long and 4–5 stitches apart. Then, using a trimmed piece of White yarn about 8in (20cm) long, make two horizontal whip stitches with a small embroidery needle where you marked the nostrils with the pins. Once complete, wrap the

embroidery needle and yarn around the horizontal nostril stitches until fully wrapped. Once finished, bring the needle back down through the head to where it entered. Knot the yarn ends together and hide them within the head.

EARS

Pinch the ears closed and pin them to the top of the head 5–6 rounds above the safety eyes, spaced evenly apart with 8 stitches between them. Angle both ears inward, with the opening to the curved ear facing forward. Once the placement is correct, whip stitch the ears onto the head using an embroidery needle by putting the needle underneath 2 stitches for the inside and outside of the side of the ear you are working on. Work around the entire ear while keeping the curved shape it was pinned in. When finished, weave in the ends.

CROCHETED MYTHICAL CREATURES

HORN

Pin the horn between the safety eyes starting at round 17–18 and ending at 14–15. Make sure to have the same number of stitches on the sides of the horn and the ears, ensuring your horn is centred and pointing upwards. With an embroidery needle, use whip stitches to attach the magic circle of the horn in place. When complete, secure and weave in the end.

HEAD AND BODY

Before attaching the head to the body, use pins to ensure the placement is correct. The neck needs to match up with the last open round of the body. Take this time to adjust the head to get the look of the unicorn you'd like, forward-facing or slightly looking to one side. Once in the right position, whip stitch the pieces together in a circle using an embroidery needle and the long tail left over from the neck. Before fully closing, add extra stuffing into the neck to support the stitching. When finished, weave in the end.

If there is a small hole where the neck connects to the whip stitches on the top of the back, use an embroidery needle and the end of the yarn to sew it closed with 2 to 3 extra whip stitches. Then weave in the end.

HAIR

Pin the hair between rounds 10 and 11 on top of the head and centre between the ears. Continue pinning the hairpiece down the back of the head and neck, staying centred. Whip stitch the hair to the head and neck with an embroidery needle and the leftover yarn tail. When finished, weave the yarn ends into the head and body.

TAIL

Pin the tail to the lower back, centred and above the thighs. Once in place, sew the tail using an embroidery needle and the leftover yarn tail to whip stitch it onto the back. Then weave the ends in the body to hide it.

UNICORN

GRIFFIN

One of the most well-known mythical creatures is the mighty griffin. A beast found in old-world legends from Asia to Greece, the griffin has the head and wings of an eagle and the body of a lion. Stories were told of how they were the protectors of riches and hoarders of gold from miners and thieves high within the mountains. Extremely wise and incredibly strong, these fierce creatures are now iconic around the world.

Skill Level

Finished size

7in (18cm)

Supplies and materials

Universal Yarn Brand Bamboo Pop DK, 50% cotton, 50% bamboo (292yd/266m per 3½oz/100g): White 101, Graphite 120, Almond 148, Sundae 139, Chocolate 152, Hickory 151, Sand 110, Penny 150

Crochet thread 10: Black and white

Hook size: 2mm

Safety eyes: 9/16in (14mm)

Polyester fibre filling

Embroidery needles

Scissors

Stitch markers

Sewing pins

Pet grooming brush

HEAD

Using White colour yarn, work all stitches in a round from bottom to top. Stuff as you crochet.

Round 1: Make a MC with 6 dc (6 sts).
Round 2: (Dc2inc) 6 times (12 sts).
Round 3: (Dc, dc2inc) 6 times (18 sts).
Round 4: (Dc, dc2inc, dc) 6 times (24 sts).
Round 5: (Dc 3, dc2inc) 6 times (30 sts).
Round 6: (Dc 2, dc2inc, dc 2) 6 times (36 sts).
Round 7: (Dc 5, dc2inc) 6 times (42 sts).
Round 8: (Dc 3, dc2inc, dc 3) 6 times (48 sts).
Round 9: (Dc 7, dc2inc) 6 times (54 sts).
Rounds 10-13: Dc in each st around (54 sts).
Round 14: (Dc 7, dc2tog) 6 times (48 sts).
Round 15: Dc 17, ch, sk, dc 12, ch, sk, dc 17 (48 sts).
Please note: The chain spaces with the skip in round 15 will be where you place the safety eyes later in the pattern.
Rounds 16-19: Dc in each st around (48 sts).
At this time, add the safety eyes in the chain spaces on round 15.
Rounds 20-21: Dc in each st around (48 sts).
Round 22: (Dc 3, dc2tog, dc 3) 6 times (42 sts).
Round 23: Dc in each st around (42 sts).
Round 24: (Dc 5, dc2tog) 6 times (36 sts).
Round 25: (Dc 2, dc2tog, dc 2) 6 times (30 sts).
Round 26: (Dc 3, dc2tog) 6 times (24 sts).
Round 27: (Dc, dc2tog, dc) 6 times (18 sts).
Round 28: (Dc, dc2tog) 6 times (12 sts).
Round 29: (Dc, dc2tog) 4 times (8 sts).
Fasten off and weave the yarn under each of the FLO, pull tight, and hide the end inside the head.

BEAK

BOTTOM BEAK

Using Graphite colour yarn, work all stitches in a round. Stuff as you crochet.

Round 1: Make a MC with 4 dc (4 sts).
Round 2: (Dc, dc2inc) twice (6 sts).
Round 3: (Dc, dc2inc, dc) twice (8 sts).
Round 4: (Dc 3, dc2inc) twice (10 sts).
Round 5: Dc 8, (dc2inc) twice (12 sts).
Round 6: Dc 8, (dc2inc) 4 times (16 sts).
Fasten off and leave a long tail for attaching.

TOP BEAK

Row 1: Ch 9, turn (9 sts).
Rows 2-3: Dc 8, ch, turn (8 sts).
Row 4: Dc 2, (dc2tog) twice, dc 2, ch, turn (6 sts).
Row 5: Dc in each st across, ch, turn (6 sts).
Row 6: Dc 2, dc2tog, dc 2, ch, turn (5 sts).
Row 7: Dc2tog, dc, dc2tog, ch, turn (3 sts).
Row 8: Dc3tog (1 st).
Fasten off and leave a long tail for attaching.

126 CROCHETED MYTHICAL CREATURES

NECK FEATHERS

Work in flat rows using White colour yarn.
When turning, always dc in the second chain from the hook, working back the other way.
Row 1: Ch 38, turn (38 sts).
Row 2: Dc in each st along, ch, turn (38 sts).
The next row will work the feathers in the FLO of round 2. When turning at the end of the chain, work the first tr in the second stitch from the hook, working back the other way up the chain.
Rows 3–14: FLO sl st, (ch 11, turn, tr in the 2nd ch from the hook, tr 9, sk 2, sl st) (23 sts) (12 feathers).
Fasten off and leave a long tail for attaching.

HEAD FEATHERS

Make two head feathers in White colour yarn, one left and one right.
Work all stitches in a flat row.
Starting in row 2, after turning, work the next stitch down the chain and rows in the third loop (see page 12); this is the loop under the stitch. This technique brings the stitches to the outside of the rows on each side.
Please note that the looser the tension, the easier it will be to grab the third loop with your hook.
Row 1: Ch 7, turn (7 sts).
Starting in the next row until the last row, remember to crochet in the third loop under the stitch.
Row 2: Sl st in 2nd ch from hook, dc 5, ch, turn (6 sts).
Row 3: Dc in the 2nd st from the hook, dc 4, ch 3, turn (8 sts).
Row 4: Sl st in the 2nd st from the hook, dc in the next ch, dc 5, ch, turn (7 sts).
Row 5: Dc in the 2nd st from the hook, dc 4, ch 3, turn (8 sts).

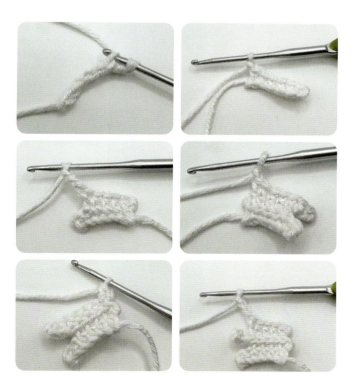

Row 6: Sl st in the 2nd st from the hook, dc in the next ch, dc 5, ch, turn (7 sts).

Row 7: Dc in the 2nd st from the hook, dc 4, ch 9, turn (14 sts).

Row 8: Sl st in 2nd ch from hook, dc 7 down the ch, dc 5, ch, turn (13 sts).

Starting with the next row, when turning on the bottom of the head feathers, the 1st dc will go in the 3rd stitch from the hook, not the 2nd.

Row 9: Dc in the 3rd st from the hook, dc 7, ch 3, turn (11 sts).

Row 10: Sl st in the 2nd st from the hook, dc in the next ch, dc 8, ch, turn (10 sts).

Row 11: Dc in the 3rd st from the hook, dc 4, ch 3, turn (8 sts).

Row 12: Sl st in the 2nd st from the hook, dc in the next ch, dc 5, ch, turn (7 sts).

Row 13: Dc in the 3rd st from the hook, dc 2, ch 3, turn (6 sts).

Row 14: Sl st in the 2nd st from the hook, dc in the next ch, dc 3 (5 sts).

For the left head feathers: With the first 6 rows on the right, fold them to the left, over the last rows. This layers the feathers to give a thicker look.
For the right head feathers: With the first 6 rows on the left, fold them to the right, over the last rows. This layers the feathers to give a thicker look.
Dc 7 stitches along the bottom edge to make a seam (7 sts). Fasten off and leave a long tail for attaching.

BODY

Using Almond colour yarn, work all stitches in a round from bottom to top. Stuff as you crochet.
Round 1: Make a MC with 6 dc (6 sts).
Round 2: (Dc2inc) 6 times (12 sts).
Round 3: (Dc, dc2inc) 6 times (18 sts).
Round 4: (Dc, dc2inc, dc) 6 times (24 sts).
Round 5: (Dc 3, dc2inc) 6 times (30 sts).
Round 6: (Dc 2, dc2inc, dc 2) 6 times (36 sts).
Round 7: (Dc 5, dc2inc) 6 times (42 sts).
Round 8: Dc in each st around (42 sts).
Round 9: (Dc 3, dc2inc, dc 3) 6 times (48 sts).
Round 10: Dc in each st around (48 sts).
Round 11: (Dc 7, dc2inc) 6 times (54 sts).
Rounds 12-20: Dc in each st around (54 sts).
Round 21: (Dc 7, dc2tog) 6 times (48 sts).
Rounds 22-25: Dc in each st around (48 sts).
Round 26: (Dc 3, dc2tog, dc 3) 6 times (42 sts).
Rounds 27-29: Dc in each st around (42 sts).
Round 30: (Dc 5, dc2tog) 6 times (36 sts).
Round 31: Dc in each st around (36 sts).
Round 32: (Dc 2, dc2tog, dc 2) 6 times (30 sts).
Round 33: (Dc 3, dc2tog) 6 times (24 sts).
Round 34: Dc in each st around (24 sts).
Round 35: Dc 10, htr 10, dc 4 (24 sts).
Fasten off and leave a long tail for attaching.

BACK LEGS

Make two legs in Almond colour yarn.
Work all stitches in a round from bottom to top. Stuff as you crochet, but do not overstuff; the top portion of the leg on one side needs to be pushed flat when sewn to the body.
Round 1: Make a MC with 6 dc (6 sts).
Round 2: (Dc2inc) 6 times (12 sts).
Round 3: (Dc, dc2inc) 6 times (18 sts).
Round 4: (Dc, dc2inc, dc) 6 times (24 sts).
Round 5: Dc 9, (PUFF, dc) 3 times, PUFF, dc 8 (24 sts).
Rounds 6-9: Dc in each st around (24 sts).
Round 10: (Dc, dc2tog, dc) 6 times (18 sts).
Round 11: Dc 7, (dc2tog) 3 times, dc 5 (15 sts).
Round 12: Dc 7, (dc2inc) 3 times, dc 4, dc2inc (19 sts).
Round 13: Dc2inc, dc 7, dc2inc, dc 3, dc2inc, dc 6 (22 sts).
Round 14: Dc 11, (dc2inc) twice, dc 9 (24 sts).
Round 15: (Dc 3, dc2inc) 6 times (30 sts).
Round 16: (Dc 2, dc2inc, dc 2) 6 times (36 sts).
Round 17: (Dc 5, dc2inc) 6 times (42 sts).
Rounds 18-19: Dc in each st around (42 sts).
Round 20: (Dc 5, dc2tog) 6 times (36 sts).
Round 21: (Dc 2, dc2tog, dc 2) 6 times (30 sts).
Round 22: Dc in each st around (30 sts).
Round 23: (Dc 3, dc2tog) 6 times (24 sts).
Round 24: Dc in each st around (24 sts).
Round 25: (Dc, dc2tog, dc) 6 times (18 sts).
Round 26: (Dc, dc2tog) 6 times (12 sts).
Round 27: (Dc, dc2tog) 4 times (8 sts).
Fasten off and weave the yarn under each of the FLO, pull tight and leave a long tail for attaching.

FRONT LEGS

FEET

Make three toes in Sundae colour yarn.
Work all stitches in a round.
Stuff the centre of the foot lightly.
Round 1: Make a MC with 6 dc (6 sts).
Rounds 2-3: Dc in each st around (6 sts).
Please note: If you are on the first or second toe, cut the yarn and fasten off, hiding the yarn ends inside the toes.
If you are on the third, do not fasten off and continue to round 4 to connect the three toes.
Round 4: With the 3rd toe still on the hook, dc 3 to the 2nd toe (leaving the next 3 dc stitches on the 2nd toe unworked), next, dc 6 around the last toe to connect all 3. Dc 3 in the unworked stitches on the back of the 2nd toe, then dc 6 around the original 3rd toe (18 sts).
Rounds 5-7: Dc in each st around (18 sts).
Round 8: (Dc, dc2tog) 6 times (12 sts).
Rounds 9-11: Dc in each st around (12 sts).
Round 12: (Dc2tog) 6 times (6 sts).
Rounds 13-14: Dc in each st around (6 sts).
Fasten off and weave the yarn under each of the FLO, then pull tight. Hide the yarn end inside the foot.
Repeat rounds 1–14 to make the second foot.

LEGS

Make two legs starting in Sundae, working all stitches in a round from bottom to top.
Leave a long yarn tail at the start to attach row 1 to the feet later in the pattern.
After row 1, work the rest of the stitches in a round.
Stuff at the end before attaching the feet.
Row 1: Ch 15 (15 sts).
Connect the 1st dc in round 2, to the 1st chain of row 1. This will make a circle to sew onto the foot later.
Rounds 2-4: Dc in each ch around (15 sts).
Round 5: (Dc 3, dc2tog) 3 times (12 sts).
Rounds 6-7: Dc in each ch around (12 sts).
Round 8: (Dc 2, dc2tog, dc 2) twice (10 sts).
Rounds 9-12: Dc in each ch around (10 sts).
Fasten off and hide the yarn tails within the legs.
Attach Almond colour yarn to the FLO of the last stitch on round 12.
Round 13: FLO (Dc2inc) 10 times (20 sts).
Round 14: FLO (Dc 2, dc2inc, dc 2) 4 times (24 sts).
Rounds 15-19: FLO dc in each ch around (24 sts).
Round 20: (Dc, dc2tog, dc) 6 times (18 sts).
Round 21: Dc in each ch around (18 sts).
Round 22: (Dc, dc2tog) 6 times (12 sts).
Pinch the legs closed and dc through both sides with 6 dc and close the opening (6 sts).
Fasten off and leave a long tail for attaching.
To complete the front legs, pin the leg to the top of the foot, starting two rounds past the toes and ending four rounds before the heel.
Make sure that the seam of 6 dc stitches is parallel with the toes before sewing the feet on. Use an embroidery needle and the leftover yarn on the leg to whip stitch (see page 21) around the bottom of the leg and connect it to the top of the foot. When it is secure, weave the extra yarn end in the foot to hide it.

WINGS

Working from top to bottom using Chocolate colour yarn, crochet two wings in rounds until instructed to work in rows. Do not stuff.

Round 1: Make a MC with 6 dc (6 sts).
Round 2: (Dc2inc) 6 times (12 sts).
Round 3: (Dc, dc2inc) 6 times (18 sts).
Rounds 4-6: Dc in each st around (18 sts).
Round 7: (Dc, dc2inc, dc) 6 times (24 sts).
Round 8: Dc in each st around (24 sts).
Round 9: Dc 9, (dc2inc) 6 times, dc 9 (30 sts).
Round 10: Dc in each st around (30 sts).

The next row will work the first set of feathers in the FLO of round 10. When turning, work the first tr in the second stitch from the hook, working back the other way up the chain.

Round 11: FLO sl st, (ch 11, turn, tr in the 2nd ch from the hook, tr 9, sk 2, sl st) 10 times (23 sts in each of 10 feathers). Do not cut the yarn; continue with round 12 on the BLO of round 10.

GRIFFIN

Round 12: BLO dc in each st around (30 sts). Change the colour to Hickory on the last stitch.
Round 13: Dc in each st around (30 sts).
Round 14: Dc 12, (dc2inc) 6 times, dc 12 (36 sts).
The next row will work the second set of feathers in the FLO of round 14. When turning, work the first tr in the second stitch from the hook, working back the other way up the chain.
Round 15: FLO sl st, (ch 11, turn, tr in the 2nd ch from the hook, tr 9, sk 2, sl st) 12 times (23 sts in each of 12 feathers). Do not cut the yarn; continue with round 16 on the BLO of round 14.
Round 16: BLO dc in each st around (36 sts). Change the colour to Sand on the last stitch.
Round 17: Dc in each st around (36 sts).

Round 18: Dc 15, (dc2inc) 6 times, dc 15 (42 sts).
The next row will work the third set of feathers in the FLO of round 18. When turning, work the first tr in the second stitch from the hook, working back the other way up the chain.
Please note: There is a break in the feathers for 5 dc stitches between feathers 6 and 7.
Round 19: FLO sl st, (ch 11, turn, tr in the 2nd ch from the hook, tr 9, sk 2, sl st) 6 times (23 sts in each of 6 feathers), dc 5 in both loops on the same round, FLO sl st, (ch 11, turn, tr in the 2nd ch from the hook, tr 9, sk 2, sl st) 6 times (23 sts in each of the 6 feathers).
Round 20 works into the BLO of round 18.
Round 20: BLO dc 19, dc 5 in both loops, BLO dc18 (42 sts). Pinch the wing closed, dc through both sides with 21 dc and close the opening (21 sts).
Fasten off and leave a long tail for attaching.

TAIL

Make the tail starting in Penny colour yarn, working in rounds from top to bottom.
Stuff as you crochet.
Round 1: Make a MC with 6 dc (6 sts).
Rounds 2-3: BLO dc in each st around (6 sts).
Round 4: BLO dc 2, (dc2inc) twice, dc 2 (8 sts).
Round 5: Dc in each st around (8 sts).
Change colour to Almond on the last stitch.
Round 6: Dc 3, (dc2inc) twice, dc 3 (10 sts).
Round 7: Dc in each st around (10 sts).
Round 8: Dc 4, (dc2inc) twice, dc 4 (12 sts).
Rounds 9-10: Dc in each st around (12 sts).
Round 11: Dc2tog, dc 3, (dc2inc) twice, dc 3, dc2tog (12 sts).
Rounds 12-13: Dc in each st around (12 sts).
Round 14: Dc2tog, dc 3, (dc2inc) twice, dc 3, dc2tog (12 sts).
Rounds 15-16: Dc in each st around (12 sts).
Round 17: Dc2tog, dc 3, (dc2inc) twice, dc 3, dc2tog (12 sts).
Rounds 18-19: Dc in each st around (12 sts).
Round 20: Dc2tog, dc 3, (dc2inc) twice, dc 3, dc2tog (12 sts).
Rounds 21-22: Dc in each st around (12 sts).
Round 23: Dc2tog, dc 3, (dc2inc) twice, dc 3, dc2tog (12 sts).
Rounds 24-25: Dc in each st around (12 sts).
Round 26: Dc2tog, dc 3, (dc2inc) twice, dc 3, dc2tog (12 sts).
Rounds 27-28: Dc in each st around (12 sts).
Round 29: Dc2tog, dc 3, (dc2inc) twice, dc 3, dc2tog (12 sts).
Rounds 30-31: Dc in each st around (12 sts).
Round 32: (Dc 5, dc2inc) twice (14 sts).
The next two rows will be worked on the top of the tail. When turning, htr in the second stitch from the hook, working back the other way.
Row 33: Htr 7, ch 2, turn (7 sts are unworked) (7 sts).
Row 34: Htr 7, ch 2, turn (7 sts)
Row 35: Htr 7 (7 sts).
Fasten off and leave a long tail for attaching.
Next, add the hair to the end of the tail by using the loop and hook method (see page 22). Start by cutting 18 strands of Penny colour yarn, 5in (12.5cm) long. Begin adding each strand of yarn on the FLO of the 1st round. Continue adding the yarn strands on the FLO of rounds 3 and 5.

Once all the hair is complete, trim the hair with scissors to 1½in (4 cm) in length. Use a pet grooming brush to brush out the hair strands to create a fluffy look. Then take the scissors and cut the sides of the hair at an upward angle to shape the end of the tail to look more rounded.

ATTACHING PIECES AND ASSEMBLY

EYES
Details on how to outline the safety eyes in crochet thread can be found in the Finishing Touches section (see page 22).

BEAK
Using pins, secure the lower beak with the increased stitches on the bottom between the safety eyes, starting at rounds 13–14 and ending at round 9. Leave about 3–4 stitches between each safety eye and the sides of the beak. With an embroidery needle and the leftover yarn tail, whip stitch the lower beak in place. Enter the needle through the face right under the bottom right corner of the beak, up through the first stitch, and back down through the face. Then continue whip stitching around the lower beak until it is sewn to the face. Once finished, weave in the yarn end and hide it within the head.

Pin the upper beak on the top of the lower, with the sides even. Once positioned straight, use an embroidery needle to whip stitch the back of the beak to the centre of the face. Weave in the leftover yarn ends in the head.

HEAD FEATHERS
Pin the head feathers on the sides of the head between rounds 18 and 24 spaced evenly apart, and angle the feathers upwards. The bottom of the feathers will be 7–8 stitches away from the safety eyes. Make sure to put the right and left pieces on the correct sides. The first smaller feathers lapping the last should be on the outside. When pinned evenly, whip stitch on using the leftover yarn tails and an embroidery needle. Weave the extra tails into the head once the ears are secured.

NECK FEATHERS

Flip the head upside down and pin the neck feathers between rounds 6 and 7 with the centre space of the feathers 6 and 7 under the beak, ensuring that the total stitches of the round of feathers and the round of the bottom of the head match up. Once pinned, use mattress stitch (see page 21) to attach the feathers to the head with the leftover yarn tails and an embroidery needle.

Weave the extra yarn tails into the head once the neck feathers are secured.

BACK AND FRONT LEGS

Tilt the body forward with the htr from the last round on the bottom, and pin the flat portion of the legs to the sides of the body starting between rounds 25 and 26. At the widest part of the legs, leave 16 stitches between them on the front and back of the body. With the legs pinned, the feet should be down and parallel to the surface. If the body is sitting, whip stitch using an embroidery needle around the large thigh part of the legs only. If not, adjust the legs up or down to ensure a good sitting position.

Add 1–2 extra whip stitches to the inside of the foot and round 9 of the body to keep the legs secure. When finished, weave in the ends.

Pin the front legs between rounds 29 and 30 of the body with approximately 4 stitches between the top of the legs. Add an extra pin to the inside of the legs near the colour change to keep them in place for sewing. If they are even, touching the surface and the body is still sitting, whip stitch the arms to the body using an embroidery needle. If not, adjust the arms up or down to ensure a good placement.

Add 2–3 whip stitches to the lower back and inside of the arms near the colour change to secure the legs against the body. If after sewing the front legs are not sitting flat on the surface, you could add a whip stitch to the heel of the foot and rounds 6–7 of the body. This ensures that the body will sit properly if needed. When the front legs are in place and stable, weave in the ends.

HEAD AND BODY

Before attaching the head to the body, pin the neck feathers to the head to keep them out of the way for sewing. Then pin the body to the head between rounds 4 and 5. Make sure that the beak is centred between the arms. Once aligned and centred, whip stitch the pieces together in a circle using an embroidery needle and the long tail left over from the body. When finished, weave in the end.

WINGS

Pin the wings from the spaced section of the third round of the feathers to the back between rounds 26–30 with approximately 3 stitches between them. The height of the wings needs to be even. Take this time to adjust their position up or down 1–2 stitches before sewing, if needed. Use an embroidery needle and the long leftover yarn ends from the wings to whip stitch along the edge of the spaced sections of each wing. Move from the corner of the bottom seam and up 4–5 rounds of the wings until the next colour.

Bring an embroidery needle down through the body to the corner of the finishing seam and whip stitch 5 stitches between rounds 26 and 27 to secure the wings. When you have finished sewing, weave the ends into the body.

TAIL

The tail should be pinned to get the correct placement before sewing. It should be attached on the lower back starting between rounds 5 and 6 and ending between rounds 12 and 13. Centre the tail with the last rows of htr stitches to the left and the tip of the tail to the right. The tail should lay across the flat surface. Once in place, use an embroidery needle and the leftover yarn tail to whip stitch the tail onto the back. Then weave the end in the body to hide it.

GRIFFIN

MERMAID

Mermaids are hybrid creatures with beautiful human features and fish tails. They have been a part of mythology for thousands of years, with many stories coming from the ancient Greeks and Romans. Mermaids are said to have magical powers with which they can control the waters, grant wishes and possibly heal the sick and wounded. Although intrigued by and curious about their cousins who walk on land, they are also cautious about humans and tend to watch them from afar.

Skill Level

Finished size

10in (25cm)

Supplies and materials

Universal Yarn Brand Bamboo Pop DK, 50% cotton, 50% bamboo (292yd/266m per 3½oz/100g): Almond 148, Ocean 107, Midnight Blue 111, Turquoise 106, Tropical Green 124, Sundae 139, Bubblegum 141, White 101, Winter Blue 126

Crochet thread 10:
Black and white

Hook size: 2mm

Safety eyes: ½in (12mm)

Polyester fibre filling

Embroidery needles

Sewing pins

Stitch markers

Scissors

Pipe cleaners

ARMS

Make two arms in Almond colour yarn.
Work all the stitches in a round from bottom to top.
Do not stuff.
Wire will be added to the arms later.

Round 1: Make a MC with 6 dc (6 sts).
Round 2: (Dc2inc) 6 times (12 sts).
Rounds 3-6: Dc in each st around (12 sts).
Round 7: Dc 4, (dc2tog) twice, dc 4 (10 sts).
Rounds 8-19: Dc in each st around (10 sts).
Fasten off and hide tails inside the arms.

TAIL

Using Ocean colour yarn, work all stitches in a round from top to bottom.
After row 1, work the rest of the stitches in a round.
Stuff the tail at the end.

Row 1: Ch 38 (38 sts).
Connect the 1st dc in round 2 to the 1st chain of row 1. This will make a circle to attach the start of the body later.
Round 2: Dc in each st around (38 sts).
Round 3: Dc 9, (dc2inc) twice, dc 17, (dc2inc) twice, dc 8 (42 sts).
Rounds 4-6: Dc in each st around (42 sts).
Round 7: Dc 9, (dc2tog) twice, dc 17, (dc2tog) twice, dc 8 (38 sts).
Rounds 8-12: Dc in each st around (38 sts).
Round 13: Dc 10, dc2tog, dc 17, dc2tog, dc 7 (36 sts).
Rounds 14-17: Dc in each st around (36 sts).
Round 18: Dc 6, dc2tog, dc 11, dc2tog, dc 10, dc2tog, dc 3 (33 sts).
Rounds 19-21: Dc in each st around (33 sts).
Round 22: Dc 6, dc2tog, dc 10, dc2tog, dc 9, dc2tog, dc 2 (30 sts).
Rounds 23-25: Dc in each st around (30 sts).
Round 26: Dc 4, dc2tog, dc 6, (dc2tog, dc 5) twice, dc2tog, dc 2 (26 sts).
Round 27: Dc in each st around (24 sts).
Round 28: Dc 7, (dc2tog) twice, dc 15 (24 sts).
Rounds 29-30: Dc in each st around (24 sts).
Round 31: Dc 6, (dc2tog) twice, dc 14 (22 sts).
Round 32: Dc in each st around (22 sts).
Round 33: Dc 5, (dc2tog) twice, dc 13 (20 sts).
Round 34: Dc in each st around (20 sts).
Round 35: Dc 4, (dc2tog) twice, dc 12 (18 sts).
Rounds 36-39: Dc in each st around (18 sts).
Round 40: (Dc, dc2tog) 6 times (12 sts).
Rounds 41-46: Dc in each st around (12 sts).
Pinch the tail closed, dc through both sides with 6 dc, and close the opening (6 sts).
Fasten off and weave the leftover yarn tail inside the body.
Add stuffing in small amounts until the tail is firmly packed and almost full.
Fasten off row 1 on the back of the top of the tail.

CROCHETED MYTHICAL CREATURES

BODY

Attach Almond colour yarn to the back of the tail, centred, on row 1 in the third loop (see page 12), leaving the FLO from row 1 unworked.

Round 1: Dc in each st around (38 sts).
Round 2: Dc 9, dc2tog, dc 17, dc2tog, dc 8 (36 sts).
Round 3: (Dc 2, dc2tog, dc 2) 6 times (30 sts).
Rounds 4–11: Dc in each st around (30 sts).

At this point, you will begin to add the arms. Remember that not everyone's tension is the same. When you add the left and right arms, if they are not parallel with the sides of the tail, add or subtract 1–2 stitches before their placement. Then adjust the starting point of the stitch marker to accommodate the extra stitches.

Round 12: Dc 6, dc 5 (place the 1st arm at the side of the body and stitch the body and arm together with the next 5 stitches. The hook will go through both the arm and the body, leaving the outside 5 stitches of the arm alone. Make sure the decreases from round 7 on the arms are facing forward), dc 11, dc 5 (place the 2nd arm at the side of the body and stitch the body and arm together with the next 5 stitches, leaving the outside 5 stitches of the arm alone. Make sure the decreases from round 7 on the arms are facing forward), dc 3 (30 sts).
Round 13: Dc 6, dc 5 (dc the 5 stitches along the outside of the 1st arm), dc 11, dc 5 (dc the 5 stitches along the outside of the 2nd arm), dc 3 (30 sts).
Round 14: Dc in each st around (30 sts).

Take two pipe cleaners and twist them together to make one thick pipe cleaner. Take the two ends and twist them together to make a point. Bring the bottom centre of the pipe cleaners up to the twist. This will create two long wires that you will feed down through both of the arms. Push the wire down in the first arm and then into the second arm. This will leave the ends of the wire coming up out of the neck.

Round 15: (Dc 3, dc2tog) 6 times (24 sts).
Round 16: (Dc, dc2tog, dc) 6 times (18 sts).
Round 17: (Dc 2, dc2tog, dc 2) 3 times (15 sts).
Round 18: Dc in each st around (15 sts).

Do not cut the yarn and continue to round 19 to make the head.

MERMAID

HEAD

Round 19: FLO (dc 2, dc2inc, dc 2) 3 times (18 sts).
Round 20: FLO (dc, dc2inc, dc) 6 times (24 sts).
Round 21: FLO (dc 3, dc2inc) 6 times (30 sts).
Round 22: (Dc 2, dc2inc, dc 2) 6 times (36 sts).
Round 23: (Dc 5, dc2inc) 6 times (42 sts).
Round 24: (Dc 3, dc2inc, dc 3) 6 times (48 sts).
Round 25: (Dc 7, dc2inc) 6 times (54 sts).
Round 26: (Dc 4, dc2inc, dc 4) 6 times (60 sts).
Rounds 27–30: Dc in each st around (60 sts).
Round 31: Dc 28, ch, sk, dc 12, ch, sk, dc 18 (60 sts).
Please note: The chain spaces with the skip in round 31 will be where you place the safety eyes later in the pattern. The chain spaces should be lining up with the armpits of the doll. If they are not, adjust them left or right by a few stitches to get the correct placement, remembering to have 12 dc between each chain space.
Rounds 32–34: Dc in each st around (60 sts).
Round 35: (Dc 4, dc2tog, dc 4) 6 times (54 sts).
At this time, add the safety eyes in the chain spaces on round 31.
Round 36: (Dc 7, dc2tog) 6 times (48 sts).
Round 37: Dc in each st around (48 sts).
Round 38: (Dc 3, dc2tog, dc 3) 6 times (42 sts).
Round 39: (Dc 5, dc2tog) 6 times (36 sts).
Round 40: (Dc 2, dc2tog, dc 2) 6 times (30 sts).
Round 41: (Dc 3, dc2tog) 6 times (24 sts).
Round 42: (Dc, dc2tog, dc) 6 times (18 sts).
Round 43: (Dc, dc2tog) 6 times (12 sts).
Round 44: (Dc, dc2tog) 4 times (8 sts).
Fasten off and weave the yarn under each of the FLO, pull tight, and hide the end inside the head.

FINNED EARS

Make two ears in Almond colour yarn.
Work all the stitches in a round, then work in rows when instructed.

Round 1: Make a MC with 9 dc, ch, turn (9 sts).
When turning and working back the other way, place the sl st in the second st from the hook. Then work the next stitches down the chain or up the row in the third loop (see page 12).
Please note that the looser the tension, the easier it will be to grab the third loop in each row with your hook.

Row 2: Dc 3, ch 5, turn, sl st, dc 3, dc in the next st on round 1 of the MC, ch, turn (4 sts).

Row 3: Sl st, dc 3, ch 2, turn, sl st, dc 4, dc in the next st on round 1 of the MC, ch, turn (9 sts).

Row 4: Sl st, dc 4, ch 2, turn, sl st, dc 5, dc 4 along round 1 of the MC (11 sts).

Fasten off and do not close the MC; leave it open with long tails to attach to the head.

MERMAID

TAIL FINS

Make two fins in Midnight Blue colour yarn, working all the stitches in a flat row.

After each row, turn and work back the other way, placing the first dc in the 2nd st from the hook.

Row 1: Ch 14, turn (14 sts).
Row 2: Dc in each ch across, ch, turn (13 sts).
Row 3: FLO dc 12, (dc 3) in the last st, ch, turn (15 sts).
Row 4: FLO dc in each st across, ch, turn (15 sts).
Row 5: FLO dc 14, (dc 3) in the last st, ch, turn (17 sts).
Row 6: FLO dc in each st across, ch, turn (17 sts).
Row 7: FLO dc 16, (dc 3) in the last st, ch, turn (19 sts).
Row 8: FLO dc in each st across, ch, turn (19 sts).
Row 9: FLO dc 18, (dc 3) in the last st, ch, turn (21 sts).
Row 10: FLO dc in each st across, ch, turn (21 sts).
Row 11: FLO dc 20, (dc 3) in the last st, ch, turn (23 sts).
Row 12: FLO dc in each st across (23 sts).

Fasten off and leave a long tail for attaching.

Weave an embroidery needle with the long yarn tail, in and out of the bottom of the fin every 3-4 rows, to make three pleats. Pull tight to scrunch the pleats on both fins and tie off. Then, with one of the yarn ends, whip stitch (see page 21) the bottom centre 3 stitches together to connect the two fins. Weave the needle through the back of the whip stitches to fasten off. Last, leave the long yarn tails for attaching the finished fin to the end of the tail.

SHELLS

Work two shells in rounds using Midnight Blue colour yarn.

Round 1: Make a MC with 6 dc, ch, turn (6 sts).
Round 2: Htr, tr2inc, (dtr2inc) twice, tr2inc, htr2inc (11 sts).

Fasten off and leave a long tail for sewing.

WAISTBAND

Work in a round using Ocean colour yarn.

Turn the doll upside down and attach the yarn with a sl st to the FLO of round 1 of the back of the tail.

Round 1: FLO dc 38, join with a sl st, ch 2 (38 sts).
Round 2: Tr 18, htr, sl st 2, htr, tr 16 (38 sts).

Fasten off, tie the two ends together and weave the yarn ends inside the tail.

HAIR

Work in rounds until instructed to work in chains.
Work the first set of hair in Turquoise colour yarn.
Round 1: Make a MC with 6 dc (6 sts).
Round 2: (Dc2inc) 6 times (12 sts).
Round 3: (Dc, dc2inc) 6 times (18 sts).
Round 4: (Dc, dc2inc, dc) 6 times (24 sts).
Work the next rows in chains to create the hair strands. Then sl st to the next stitch in round 4 before starting the next row. After turning and working back the other way, place the first dc in the second st from the hook. Then the rest of the stitches need to be worked in the third loop (see page 12).
Row 1: Ch 25, turn, dc 24 up the ch, sl st (24 sts) (1 hair strand).
Rows 2–18: Ch 25, turn, dc 24 up the ch, sl st (24 sts) (17 rows of hair strands).
Leave the last six stitches unworked.
Fasten off and leave a long tail for sewing.
The second set of hair is worked in Tropical Green colour yarn.
Round 1: Make a MC with 6 dc (6 sts).
Round 2: (Dc2inc) 6 times (12 sts).
Round 3: (Dc, dc2inc) 6 times (18 sts).
Work the next part in chains to create the hair strands. Then sl st a colour change to the next st in round 3 before starting the next row.
After turning and working back the other way, place the first dc in the seond st from the hook. Then the rest of the stitches need to be worked in the third loop.
Rows 1–5: Ch 23, turn, dc 22 up the ch, sl st (22 sts) (5 rows of hair strands).
Rows 6–7: Ch 32, turn, dc 31 up the ch, sl st (31 sts) (2 rows of hair strands).
Rows 8–11: Ch 11, turn, dc 10 up the ch, sl st (10 sts) (4 rows of hair strands).
Rows 12–13: Ch 32, turn, dc 31 up the ch, sl st (31 sts) (2 rows of hair strands).
Rows 14–18: Ch 23, turn, dc 22 up the ch, sl st (22 sts) (5 rows of hair strands).
Fasten off and leave a long tail for sewing.

STARFISH

Make three starfish in Sundae colour yarn.
Work all the stitches in a round.
Round 1: Make a MC with 10 dc (10 sts).
Round 2: (Htr, ch 3, dc in the 3rd ch from hook, htr in the same st, sl st) 5 times (35 sts) (5 points).
Fasten off, tie both yarn ends together and leave a long tail for attaching.

MERMAID

ATTACHING PIECES AND ASSEMBLY

EYES
Details on how to outline the safety eyes in crochet thread can be found in the Finishing Touches section (see page 22).

NOSE AND CHEEKS
Using pins, mark the width of the nose in the centre of the face between rounds 29 and 30 and 3 stitches apart. Using Almond colour yarn, with an embroidery needle enter the yarn through the side of the head to the first nose pin. Whip stitch a nose at the two pins 4–5 times. Once complete, exit the yarn back through the same stitch on the side of the head, knot the two ends, and weave the ends into the head.

Using Bubblegum colour yarn, whip stitch or embroider a double line beginning on the round below the safety eyes, starting near the end of the safety eye and 3 stitches wide. Enter your thread through the bottom of the head and embroider the cheeks. Once finished, bring the needle back down through the head to where it entered. Knot the thread ends together and hide them within the head.

FINNED EARS

Pin the ears on the side of the head between rounds 28 and 32 with the fins pointing upwards. Have about 31 stitches between the bottom of the ears along the front of the head. When pinned evenly, sew on using the leftover ends and an embroidery needle. Then add 1–2 extra whip stitches to the bottom of the ear to secure it to the head. Weave the extra yarn ends into the head.

TAIL FIN

The fin should be pinned in three spots before sewing – the centre and the two sides – to line up the sides of the fin and the seam of 6 dc stitches from closing the tail. Since all of the leftover yarn ends are in the centre of the fin, use an embroidery needle to weave a yarn end through the lower back of the fin to get the needle to the side. Then whip stitch the large fin to the seam of the tail. Use multiple whip stitches if necessary to get the fin to attach firmly. When secure, weave all the extra yarn ends into the tail.

MERMAID

SEA SHELLS

Each of the shells needs to be pinned to get the right placement before attaching. Pin the bottom of the shells to the front of the body at round 8 and the top of the shell at round 13 or 14. The shells should be even, facing the same side, and either touching or with half a stitch between them. Using an embroidery needle and the long yarn end, whip stitch 4 stitches around each of the shells – at the top, bottom and both sides of the shells. Once the shells are sewn and securely attached, weave both of the yarn ends through the back of the body, tie the ends together and hide them inside the mermaid.

ATTACHING THE HAIR

Match up the MC of the first larger hair piece and the MC of the head and add a pin to the top of the hair to keep it in place. The 6 unworked stitches on round 4 need to be centred between the safety eyes.

Pin approximately 13 of the hair strands to the back of the head, side by side, to cover it. Twist every other hair strand once to add texture to the back of the hair. Adjust the hair strands as needed to fill any bare spots.

Sew the hair using the embroidery needle and the long tail left over from making the hair. Starting at the top of the hair, make a few whip stitches around some of the stitches on the outside rounds. Make sure to go through both the hair and the head to keep the hair from moving around. Next, flip the head upside down and sew the hair strands down beginning at the pins along the back hair strands and working your way around the back of the head.

Next, match up the MC of the second smaller hair piece and the MC of the first hair piece and add a pin to the top to keep it in place. The four shorter hair strands need to be centred between the safety eyes and pinned side by side above the right safety eye. Leave the four longer hair strands, paired in front of the two ears. Twist the last ten hair strands and pin them to the back of the head, overlapping the other sewn hair strands. Adjust the hair strands as needed to fill any bare spots.

Then sew the smaller hair piece on with the same steps as the first hair piece, making sure the embroidery needle goes through both hair pieces when whip stitching along the outside rounds. Once round 4 is attached, bring the needle down to the shorter hair strands and whip stitch the ends of them to the head. Whip stitch the extra hair strands from the first, larger hair piece down around the two ears. Then twist the longer, side hair strands from the second hair piece in front of the ears and whip stitch to the other lower hair strand if necessary. Hide all the yarn tails inside the head to complete attaching the hair pieces.

STARFISH

Sew the starfish on the hair in the front where it parts. Use an embroidery needle and the leftover yarn tails to whip stitch the starfish to the head. Once finished, tie the two yarn ends from the starfish together tightly, then weave each end into the head.

SPOTS

Mark clusters of spots on the tail with pins. Then, alternating between White and Winter Blue colour yarn, enter the large embroidery needle through the tail and exit a few stitches from where you want the spots. Tie a knot at the bottom of the yarn where it exits the tail. Insert the embroidery needle 1 stitch over from the knot. Repeat this for at least 12–15 more spots depending on how and where you want them. Exit the embroidery needle through the tail and out where it entered, tie off and hide the ends inside the tail. You also have the option of using two or three different colours for the spots.

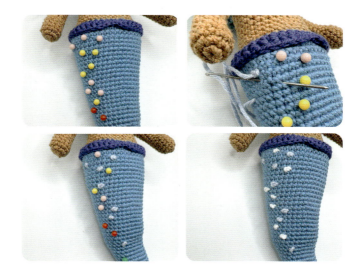

WOLPERTINGER

The wolpertinger is a small, mythical woodland creature from the alpine forests of Bavaria, with the body of a rabbit, the antlers of a deer and the wings of a pheasant. Prone to falling in love with human females, the wolpertinger is known to trick unsuspecting tourists into losing their way in the dark forests.

Skill Level

Finished size

7in (18cm)

Supplies and materials

Universal Yarn Brand Bamboo Pop DK, 50% cotton, 50% bamboo (292yd/266m per 3½oz/100g): Sand 110, Rosy 143, Darling Pink 125, Hickory 151, Almond 148, Winter Squash 129, Apricot Slush 135

Crochet thread:
Black and white

Hook size: 2mm

Safety eyes: ½in (12mm)

Polyester fibre filling

Embroidery needles

Scissors

Stitch markers

Sewing pins

Pompom (optional)

HEAD

Using Sand colour yarn, work all stitches in a round from bottom to top. Stuff as you crochet.

Round 1: Make a MC with 6 dc (6 sts).
Round 2: (Dc2inc) 6 times (12 sts).
Round 3: (Dc, dc2inc) 6 times (18 sts).
Round 4: (Dc, dc2inc, dc) 6 times (24 sts).
Round 5: (Dc 3, dc2inc) 6 times (30 sts).
Round 6: (Dc 2, dc2inc, dc 2) 6 times (36 sts).
Round 7: (Dc 5, dc2inc) 6 times (42 sts).
Round 8: (Dc 3, dc2inc, dc 3) 6 times (48 sts).
Round 9: (Dc 7, dc2inc) 6 times (54 sts).
Rounds 10–13: Dc in each st around (54 sts).
Round 14: (Dc 7, dc2tog) 6 times (48 sts).
Round 15: (Dc 3, dc2tog, dc 3) 6 times (42 sts).
Round 16: Dc 15, ch, sk, dc 10, ch, sk, dc 15 (42 sts).
Please note: The chain spaces with the skip in round 16 will be where you place the safety eyes later in the pattern.
Round 17: Dc in each st around (42 sts).
Round 18: (Dc 3, dc2inc, dc 3) 6 times (48 sts).
Round 19: Dc in each st around (48 sts).
Round 20: (Dc 3, dc2tog, dc 3) 6 times (42 sts).
Round 21: (Dc 5, dc2tog) 6 times (36 sts).
Rounds 22–23: Dc in each st around (36 sts).
At this time, add the safety eyes in the chain spaces on round 16.
Round 24: (Dc 2, dc2tog, dc 2) 6 times (30 sts).
Round 25: Dc in each st around (30 sts).
Round 26: (Dc 3, dc2tog) 6 times (24 sts).
Round 27: (Dc, dc2tog, dc) 6 times (18 sts).
Round 28: (Dc, dc2tog) 6 times (12 sts).
Round 29: (Dc, dc2tog) 4 times (8 sts).
Fasten off and weave the yarn under each of the FLO, pull tight, and hide the end inside the head.

BODY

Using Sand colour yarn, work all stitches in a round from bottom to top. Stuff as you crochet.

Round 1: Make a MC with 6 dc (6 sts).
Round 2: (Dc2inc) 6 times (12 sts).
Round 3: (Dc, dc2inc) 6 times (18 sts).
Round 4: (Dc, dc2inc, dc) 6 times (24 sts).
Round 5: (Dc 3, dc2inc) 6 times (30 sts).
Round 6: (Dc 2, dc2inc, dc 2) 6 times (36 sts).
Round 7: (Dc 5, dc2inc) 6 times (42 sts).
Round 8: (Dc 3, dc2inc, dc 3) 6 times (48 sts).
Rounds 9–13: Dc in each st around (48 sts).
Round 14: (Dc 3, dc2tog, dc 3) 6 times (42 sts).
Rounds 15–17: Dc in each st around (42 sts).
Round 18: (Dc 5, dc2tog) 6 times (36 sts).

Rounds 19-21: Dc in each st around (36 sts).
Round 22: (Dc 2, dc2tog, dc 2) 6 times (30 sts).
Rounds 23-24: Dc in each st around (30 sts).
Round 25: (Dc 3, dc2tog) 6 times (24 sts).
Rounds 26-28: Dc in each st around (24 sts).
Round 29: BLO dc in each st around (24 sts).
Fasten off and leave a long tail for attaching.

COLLAR
Attach Rosy colour yarn to the FLO of round 28 on the back side of the body.
Round 1: FLO dc in each st around, join to the first stitch with a sl st (24 sts).
Flip the body upside down and work in the opposite direction for the next round.
Work the first htr in the 3rd stitch from the hook.
Round 2: Ch 2, htr in each st around, join to the first stitch with a sl st (24 sts).
Round 3: Ch 2, htr 7, tr 4, tr2inc, (tr, ch 3, turn and dc in the 3rd ch from hook, tr) in the same st, tr2inc, tr 4, htr 6, sl st (31 sts).
Fasten off and leave a long tail for sewing.

ARMS
Make two arms in Sand colour yarn, working all stitches in a round from bottom to top.
Stuff as you crochet.
Round 1: Make a MC with 6 dc (6 sts).
Round 2: (Dc2inc) 6 times (12 sts).
Rounds 3-5: Dc in each st around (12 sts).
Round 6: (Dc2inc) 3 times, dc 3, (dc2tog) twice, dc 2 (13 sts).
Round 7: Dc in each st around (13 sts).
Round 8: Dc 3, dc2inc, dc 9 (14 sts).
Rounds 9-12: Dc in each st around (14 sts).
Round 13: Dc 4, (dc2tog) twice, dc 4, (dc2inc) twice (14 sts).
Round 14: Dc 10, (dc2inc) twice, dc 2 (16 sts).
Rounds 15-17: Dc in each st around (16 sts).
Round 18: Dc 12, dc2tog, dc 2 (15 sts).
Round 19: (Dc 3, Dc2tog) 3 times (12 sts).
Pinch the arms closed. If your seam is not centred with the increases and decreases being on the top and bottom of the arm, add 1-3 stitches.
Dc through both sides with 6 dc and close the opening (6 sts).
Fasten off and leave a long tail for attaching.

WOLPERTINGER

BACK LEGS

Make two legs starting in Rosy colour yarn.
Work all stitches in a round from bottom to top.
Stuff as you crochet, but do not overstuff. The top portion of the leg needs to be pushed flat when sewn to the body.
Round 1: Ch 9, turn (working around the ch), dc2inc in the 2nd ch from hook, dc 6, dc 4 in the next st, dc 6, dc2inc (20 sts).
Round 2: (Dc 9, dc2inc) twice (22 sts).
Round 3: Dc 8, (PUFF, dc) twice, PUFF, dc 9 (22 sts). Change colour to Sand.
Round 4: FLO dc in each st around (22 sts).
Round 5: Dc 8, (dc2tog) 3 times, dc 8 (19 sts).
Round 6: Dc 7, (dc2tog) twice, dc 8 (17 sts).
Round 7: Dc 6, (dc2tog) twice, dc 7 (15 sts).
Round 8: Dc 6, (dc2inc) 3 times, dc 5, dc2inc (19 sts).
Round 9: Dc2inc, dc 6, dc2inc, dc 2, dc2inc, dc 8 (22 sts).
Round 10: Dc 10, (dc2inc) twice, dc 10 (24 sts).
Round 11: (Dc 3, dc2inc) 6 times (30 sts).
Round 12: (Dc 2, dc2inc, dc 2) 6 times (36 sts).
Rounds 13–14: Dc in each st around (36 sts).
Round 15: (Dc 2, dc2tog, dc 2) 6 times (30 sts).
Round 16: (Dc 3, dc2tog) 6 times (24 sts).
Round 17: (Dc, dc2tog, dc) 6 times (18 sts).
Round 18: (Dc, dc2tog) 6 times (12 sts).
Fasten off and weave the yarn under each of the FLO, pull tight and leave a long tail for attaching.

MUZZLE

Using Rosy colour yarn, work all stitches in a round in the magic circle.
Round 1: Make a MC with ch 2, dtr 3, tr 4, dtr 3, ch 2, sl st (20 sts).
Fasten off and leave a long tail for attaching.

EARS

Make two ears starting in Sand colour yarn, then change colours when instructed.
Work all the stitches in a round.
Do not stuff.
Round 1: Make a MC with 6 dc (6 sts).
Round 2: Dc in each st around (6 sts).
Round 3: (Dc2inc) 6 times (12 sts).
Change colour to Darling Pink (colour B) when instructed.
Round 4: Dc 11, dc in colour B (12 sts).
Round 5: Dc in colour B, dc 10, dc in colour B (12 sts).
Round 6: Dc in colour B, dc2inc in colour B, (dc, dc2inc) 4 times, dc, dc2inc in colour B (18 sts).
Rounds 7–9: Dc 3 in colour B, dc 13, dc 2 in colour B (18 sts).
Round 10: Dc 3 in colour B, dc 4, (dc2tog) twice, dc 5, dc 2 in colour B (16 sts).

Round 11: Dc 3 in colour B, dc 3, (dc2tog) twice, dc 4, dc 2 in colour B (14 sts).
Round 12: Dc 3 in colour B, dc 2, (dc2tog) twice, dc 3, dc 2 in colour B (12 sts).
Rounds 13-14: Dc 3 in colour B, dc 7, dc 2 in colour B (12 sts).
Round 14: Dc 3 in colour B, dc 7 (10 sts).
Leave the rest of the stitches in round 14 unworked. Pinch the ear closed, dc through both sides with 5 dc, and close the opening (5 sts).
Fasten off and leave a long tail for attaching.

Round 8: Dc in each st around (12 sts).
Round 9: Dc 4, dc2inc, dc 5, dc2inc, dc (14 sts).
Rounds 10-11: Dc in each st around (14 sts).
Round 12: Dc 3, (dc2tog) twice, dc 3, (dc2inc) twice, dc 2 (14 sts).
Fasten off and leave a long tail for attaching.

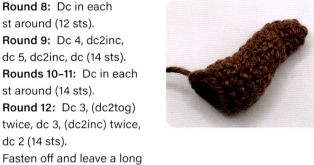

ANTLER POINTS

Make two points with Hickory colour yarn.
Work all the stitches in a round.
Do not stuff.
Round 1: Make a MC with 4 dc (4 sts).
Round 2: Dc in each st around (4 sts).
Round 3: (Dc, dc2inc) twice (6 sts).
Fasten off and leave a long tail for attaching.
Pin the small point to the large antler between rounds 6 and 8 on the outward curve. Using an embroidery needle and the leftover yarn tail, whip stitch (see page 21) the two pieces together to make the full antler. Repeat these steps for the second antler.

ANTLERS

Make two antlers with Hickory colour yarn.
Work all the stitches in a round.
Stuff as you go.
Round 1: Make a MC with 6 dc (6 sts).
Round 2: (Dc 2, dc2inc) twice (8 sts).
Round 3: Dc in each st around (8 sts).
Round 4: (Dc 3, dc2inc) twice (10 sts).
Round 5: (Dc2inc) twice, dc 2, (dc2tog) twice, dc 2 (10 sts).
Round 6: Dc in each st around (10 sts).
Round 7: Dc 2, (dc2inc) twice, dc 6 (12 sts).

WOLPERTINGER

WINGS

Make two wings working in flat rows starting with the Hickory colour yarn.

When turning, always dc in the second stitch or chain from the hook, working back the other way. The chains on the end of the row do not count as stitches.

Row 1: Ch 14, turn (14 sts).
Row 2: Dc in each st across, ch, turn (13 sts).
Row 3: Dc2inc, (dc 5, dc2inc) twice, ch, turn (16 sts).
Row 4: Dc2inc, dc 6, dc2inc, dc 7, dc2inc, ch, turn (19 sts).
Row 5: Dc2inc, (dc 8, dc2inc) twice, ch, turn (22 sts).
Row 6: Dc2inc, dc 9, dc2inc, dc 10, dc2inc, ch, turn (25 sts).

The next row will create a feather-like texture on the FLO on the previous rows. Work all stitches in the FLO.

Row 7: (FLO dc, tr, (dtr 5) in the next st, tr) 6 times, dc (49 sts).

Fasten off and hide the end inside the wing.
Flip the wing upside down and attach the Almond colour yarn to the BLO of the first st on round 6 of the wing.

Row 8: BLO dc in each st across, ch, turn (25 sts).
Rows 9–10: Dc in each st across, ch, turn (25 sts).

The next row will create a feather-like texture on the FLO on the previous rows. Work all stitches in the FLO.

Row 11: (FLO dc, tr, (dtr 5) in the next st, tr) 6 times, dc (49 sts).

Fasten off and hide the end inside the wing.
Flip the wing upside down and attach the Winter Squash colour yarn to the BLO of the first st on round 10 of the wing.

Row 12: BLO dc in each st across, ch, turn (25 sts).
Rows 13–14: Dc in each st across, ch, turn (25 sts).

The next row will create a feather-like texture on the FLO on the previous rows. Work all stitches in the FLO.

Row 15: (FLO dc, tr, (dtr 5) in the next st, tr) 6 times, dc (49 sts).

Fasten off and hide the end inside the wing.
Flip the wing upside down and attach the Apricot Slush colour yarn to the BLO of the first st on round 14 of the wing.

Row 16: BLO dc in each st across, ch, turn (25 sts).
Rows 17–18: Dc in each st across, ch, turn (25 sts).

The next row will create a feather-like texture on the FLO on the previous rows. Work all stitches in the FLO.

Row 19: (FLO dc, tr, (dtr 5) in the next st, tr) 6 times, dc, ch, turn (49 sts).

Continue the Apricot Slush colour yarn and connect the next stitch to the BLO of row 18.

Row 20: BLO dc in each st across, ch, turn (25 sts).
Row 21: Dc2tog, dc 6, dc2tog, dc 5, dc2tog, dc 6, dc2tog (21 sts).
Row 22: Dc in each st across, ch, turn (21 sts).
Row 23: Work all stitches in the FLO. (FLO dc, tr, (dtr 5) in the next st, tr) 5 times, dc, ch, turn (41 sts).

Connect the next stitch to the BLO of row 22.

Row 24: BLO dc in each st across, ch, turn (21 sts).
Row 25: Dc2tog, dc 4, dc2tog, dc 5, dc2tog, dc 4, dc2tog (17 sts).
Row 26: Dc in each st across, ch, turn (17 sts).

Row 27: Work all stitches in the FLO. (FLO dc, tr, (dtr 5) in the next st, tr) 4 times, dc, ch, turn (33 sts).
Connect the next stitch to the BLO of row 26.
Row 28: BLO dc in each st across, ch, turn (17 sts).
Row 29: Dc2tog, dc 3, dc2tog, dc 3, dc2tog, dc 3, dc2tog (13 sts).
Row 30: Dc in each st across, ch, turn (13 sts).
Row 31: Work all stitches in the FLO. (FLO dc, tr, (dtr 5) in the next st, tr) 3 times, dc, ch, turn (25 sts).
Connect the next stitch to the BLO of row 30.
Row 32: BLO dc in each st across, ch, turn (13 sts).
Row 33: Dc2tog, dc 2, dc2tog, dc, dc2tog, dc 2, dc2tog (9 sts).
Row 34: Dc in each st across, ch, turn (9 sts).

Row 35: Work all stitches in the FLO. (FLO dc, tr, (dtr 5) in the next st, tr) twice, dc, ch, turn (17 sts).
Fasten off and leave a long tail for sewing.
Fold the wing in half long ways and pin it together. With the leftover yarn end, whip stitch the last two sets of 5 dtr sts together to create one feather. Then continue whip stitching up the open side of the wing until you reach the top of the first row of 5 dtr sts. Finish off and hide the yarn tail inside the wing.
Attach the Hickory colour yarn with a dc to the open side of the wing just above the last finish off from the previous instructions. With the hook, dc through both sides of the top of the wing to close the rest of the opening. Once the wing is closed, finish off and leave a long tail for attaching to the back of the body.

ATTACHING PIECES AND ASSEMBLY

EYES

Details on how to outline the safety eyes in crochet thread can be found in the Finishing Touches section (see page 22).

MUZZLE AND NOSE

Using pins, secure the muzzle to the front of the face with the point upwards starting between rounds 14 and 15, with 4 stitches between each safety eye and the sides of the muzzle. With an embroidery needle and the leftover yarn tail, whip stitch the muzzle in place. Enter the needle through the face right under the bottom centre portion of the muzzle then up through the first stitch and back down through the face. Then continue whip stitching around the muzzle until it is sewn to the face completely. Once finished, tie the yarn ends together and hide them within the head.

To create a small nose onto the muzzle, use the black crochet thread and enter the thread through the bottom of the head then out the face just above the top of the muzzle. Bring the needle down to the bottom centre portion of the muzzle and back up through the left top corner of the muzzle. This will create the line from the top of the nose to the bottom. Then bring the needle down through the centre of the magic circle and out through the top right corner of the muzzle. Continue moving your thread along the outside of the muzzle and through the magic circle to make a fan-like shape with the black thread until it is complete. Once finished, outline the top of the nose with a few whip stitches. Bring the needle down through the head, tie the thread ends together and hide them within the head.

158   CROCHETED MYTHICAL CREATURES

ANTLERS

Pin the antlers directly above the safety eyes, with the small points on the inside of the antlers. Angle them up towards the top of the head with the outside bottom rounds pinned at round 24 and 5-6 stitches spaced between each of them. When centred, use an embroidery needle and whip stitch around the edge of the antlers to attach the pieces securely. Once complete, weave in and hide the leftover tails inside the head.

EARS

Pin the ears to the top of the head between rounds 22 and 27 with the inner ear facing outwards. The side of the ear at the top of the head needs to be pinned up against the centre of the back of the antler, leaving the bottom outside edge of the ear on round 22, 3 stitches away from the antler. Both ears should be spaced apart evenly on the top of the head. Once the placement is correct, sew with an embroidery needle to attach them in place. When finished, weave in the ends.

HEAD AND BODY

Before attaching the head to the body, use pins to ensure the placement is correct. You want the collar to match up with round 4 of the head having 24 stitches each. Once aligned and centred, attach the two pieces together by using an embroidery needle and the long tail left over from the body to whip stitch the pieces together. When finished, weave in the end.

WOLPERTINGER

LEGS AND ARMS

Pin the flat portion of the legs to the sides of the body starting between rounds 20 and 21. With the legs pinned straight, the feet need to be down and parallel with the surface it is on. If the wolpertinger is sitting properly, you can start sewing around the large thigh part of the legs only. If not, take this time to adjust the legs up or down to ensure a good sitting position. When finished, weave in the end.

Flip up the collar around the neck to make space to sew the arms onto the body. The arms should be pinned 1 round down from the collar on the sides of the body. Leave at least 10 stitches between them on the back, and angle them slightly down where the arms are resting on the legs. If they are even, you can start sewing the pieces to the body. If not, take this time to adjust the arms up or down to ensure a good placement. When complete, secure and weave in the end.

160   CROCHETED MYTHICAL CREATURES

WINGS

Pin the wings to the back of the body in the space between both arms. They should be angled outwards with rows 3–6 touching in the centre of the back. Using an embroidery needle and the long leftover yarn ends from the wings, whip stitch the top of each wing to the back of the wolpertinger. When finished sewing, weave the ends into the body.

TAIL

Add a fur pompom, or make your own using the Rosy colour yarn. Cut a piece of yarn about 7in (18cm) long and set it aside. Then wrap the yarn around two fingers approximately 75 times. Taking the long piece of cut yarn, tie a knot around the yarn bundle. Carefully remove it from your fingers and lay it on the centre of the cut yarn. Flip it over, add a second knot in the back and cut through the loops on either side of the bundle. Shake gently and use your scissors to shape the pompom, cutting any longer yarn ends. Whip stitch the pompom onto the lower back between rounds 9 and 10 with an embroidery needle.

WOLPERTINGER

WATER KELPIE

Beware of the kelpie: this shape-shifting Scottish legend would appear as a beautiful tame horse to curious children at the river's edge. Once the kelpie had tricked a child to ride upon its back, it would drag the child into the deepest part of the river, never to be seen again.

Skill Level

Finished size

9in (18cm)

Supplies and materials

Universal Yarn Brand Bamboo Pop DK, 50% cotton, 50% bamboo (292yd/266m per 3½oz/100g): Blue Whisper 134, Graphite 120, Tropical Green 124, Turquoise 106, Sunny 113, Bubblegum 141

Crochet thread 10:
Black and white

Hook size: 2mm

Safety eyes: 9⁄16in (14mm)

Polyester fibre filling

Embroidery needles

Scissors

Stitch markers

Sewing pins

Pipe cleaners

WATER KELPIE

HEAD

Using Blue Whisper colour yarn, work all stitches in a round from top to bottom.
Stuff as you crochet.

Round 1: Make a MC with 6 dc (6 sts).
Round 2: (Dc2inc) 6 times (12 sts).
Round 3: (Dc, dc2inc) 6 times (18 sts).
Round 4: (Dc, dc2inc, dc) 6 times (24 sts).
Round 5: (Dc 3, dc2inc) 6 times (30 sts).
Round 6: (Dc 2, dc2inc, dc 2) 6 times (36 sts).
Round 7: (Dc 5, dc2inc) 6 times (42 sts).
Round 8: (Dc 3, dc2inc, dc 3) 6 times (48 sts).
Round 9: (Dc 7, dc2inc) 6 times (54 sts).
Round 10: (Dc 4, dc2inc, dc 4) 6 times (60 sts).
Round 11: (Dc 9, dc2inc) 6 times (66 sts).
Round 12: (Dc 5, dc2inc, dc 5) 6 times (72 sts).
Round 13: Dc 48, leaving 24 dc sts unworked (48 sts).
Place a stitch marker on the 2 unworked stitches, stitch 49 and stitch 72 of round 12. This will mark the neck section to work later in the pattern. The next set of rounds will create the head only by working around the 48 stitches of round 13. Fold the piece in half and work round 14.
Round 14: Dc in each st around (48 sts).
Round 15: (Dc 7, dc2inc) 6 times (54 sts).
Round 16: Dc in each st around (54 sts).
Round 17: (Dc 7, dc2tog) 6 times (48 sts).
Round 18: Dc 16, ch, sk, dc 16, ch, sk, dc 14 (48 sts).
Please note: The chain spaces with the skip in round 18 will be where you place the safety eyes later in the pattern.
Round 19: Dc in each st around (48 sts).
Round 20: Dc 9, dc2tog, dc 8, (dc2tog, dc) twice, dc2tog, dc 8, dc2tog, dc 9, dc2tog (42 sts).
Round 21: Dc in each st around (42 sts).
Round 22: (Dc 5, dc2tog) 6 times (36 sts).
At this time, add the safety eyes in the chain spaces on round 18.
Round 23: Dc in each st around (36 sts).
Round 24: Dc 17, (dc2tog) 3 times, dc 13 (33 sts).
Round 25: Dc 17, (dc2inc) 3 times, dc 13 (36 sts)
Round 26: (Dc 2, dc2tog, dc 2) 6 times (30 sts).
Round 27: Dc in each st around (30 sts).
At this point, if you haven't started to stuff the head, start the stuffing now.
Round 28: (Dc 3, dc2tog) 6 times (24 sts).
Round 29: (Dc, dc2tog, dc) 6 times (18 sts).
Round 30: (Dc, dc2tog) 6 times (12 sts).

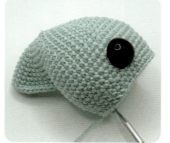

Before the last round and fastening off, add more stuffing to the snout and pack it fairly tight to maintain the shape of the head.

Round 31: (Dc, dc2tog) 4 times (8 sts).

Fasten off and weave the yarn under each of the FLO, then pull tight. Bring an embroidery needle down through the centre of the magic circle and out the bottom of the head. Pull slightly to flatten round 31 and hide the end inside the head.

NECK AND BODY

Attach the Blue Whisper colour yarn to the first stitch of the open neck at round 13 and work all stitches in a round from right to left.

Stuff as you crochet, making sure to stuff the bottom of the head and the opening of the top of the neck. The hole left over from connecting the two pieces will be closed when the body is finished.

Rounds 14–19: Dc in each st around (24 sts).
Round 20: (Dc 3, dc2inc) 6 times (30 sts).
Rounds 21–26: Dc in each st around (30 sts).

The next eight rows will be worked on the front of the body to make the front of the kelpie curve.

When turning, do not chain but dc in the second stitch from the hook, working back the other way.

Row 27: Dc 15, turn (15 sts).

In the next row, your stitches will pass the starting stitch before reaching the 24th dc.

Row 28: Dc 24, turn (24 sts).

For rows 29–33, the last stitch in each row will be left unworked before turning.

Row 29: Dc 22, turn (22 sts).
Row 30: Dc 20, turn (20 sts).
Row 31: Dc 18, turn (18 sts).
Row 32: Dc 16, turn (16 sts).
Row 33: Dc 14, turn (14 sts).
Row 34: Dc 12, turn (12 sts).

Next will be a round; do not turn after the 11 dc stitches and work the 8 dc stitches down the side of the rows. Then continue around the opening of the neck to make a full round.

Round 35: Dc 11, dc 8 down the 1st side, dc 5, dc 8 up the 2nd side (32 sts).

WATER KELPIE

The starting stitch will now be moved to the first stitch on the previous row. Make sure to move the stitch marker.

Round 36: Dc 5, dc2inc, dc 12, (dc2inc, dc 2) twice, dc2inc, dc 7 (36 sts).
Rounds 37–41: Dc in each st around (36 sts).
Round 42: (Dc 2, dc2tog) 3 times, dc 8, (dc2inc, dc 2) twice, dc2inc, dc 9 (36 sts).
Rounds 43–45: Dc in each st around (36 sts).
Rounds 46–50: Dc 3, htr 6, dc 27 (36 sts).
Rounds 51–52: Dc in each st around (36 sts).
Round 53: Dc 6, (dc2tog) twice, dc 26 (34 sts).
Rounds 54–55: Dc in each st around (34 sts).
Round 56: Dc 5, (dc2tog) twice, dc 25 (32 sts).
Rounds 57–58: Dc in each st around (32 sts).
Round 59: Dc 4, (dc2tog) twice, dc 24 (30 sts).
Round 60: Dc in each st around (30 sts).
Round 61: Dc 4, dc2tog, dc 6, (dc2tog, dc 5) twice, dc2tog, dc 2 (26 sts).
Round 62: Dc 3, (dc2tog) twice, dc 19 (24 sts).
Round 63: Dc in each st around (24 sts).
Round 64: Dc 12, FLO dc 12 (24 sts).
Round 65: Dc 2, (dc2tog) twice, dc 6, FLO 12 (22 sts).
Round 66: Dc 10, FLO dc 12 (22 sts).
Round 67: Dc, (dc2tog) twice, dc 5, FLO 12 (20 sts).

On round 68, make sure to have loose tension when working the slip stitches; this will help to get the hook underneath the FLO when working round 69.

Round 68: Dc 10, FLO sl st 10 (20 sts).
Round 69: (Dc2tog) twice, FLO dc 16 (18 sts).
Rounds 70–71: Dc 8, FLO dc 10 (18 sts).

Take two pipe cleaners, pair them together, fold them in half and twist the four ends together to make one thick pipe cleaner. Fold them in half once more until it is 2¾in (7cm) long. Then give the pipe cleaners three or four more twists to ensure there are no loose ends.

Stuff the end portion of the tail firmly, leaving a small centre hole in the stuffing. Insert the twisted pipe cleaners into the small centre hole in the stuffing of the tail and push it firmly down as far as it will go. There should be 1¾in (4.5cm) of pipe cleaner sticking out of the tail. Add extra stuffing around the pipe cleaner and the inside of the tail. Continue crocheting around the pipe cleaners.
Rounds 72-74: Dc 8, FLO dc 10 (18 sts).
Round 75: (Dc, dc2tog) 6 times (12 sts).
Rounds 76-89: Dc in each st around (12 sts).
Pinch the tail closed, dc through both sides with 6 dc and close the opening (6 sts).
Fasten off and weave the leftover yarn tail inside the body.

Where there is a hole visible where the head and neck connect, use an embroidery needle and the leftover yarn from starting round 14 to sew it closed with 3-4 whip stitches (see page 21).

LEGS
Start by making two hooves in Graphite colour yarn. Work all stitches in a round from bottom to top. Stuff as you crochet.
Round 1: Make a MC with 9 dc (9 sts).
Round 2: (Dc2inc) 9 times (18 sts).
Round 3: BLO dc in each st around (18 sts).
Rounds 4-5: Dc in each st around (18 sts).
Fasten off and weave the tails inside the rounds. Attach Blue Whisper colour yarn to the BLO of round 5 on the back side.
Round 6: BLO dc in each st around (18 sts).
Rounds 7-9: Dc in each st around (18 sts).
Rounds 10-11: Dc 7, htr 6, dc 5 (18 sts).
Round 12: (Dc2inc) 3 times, dc 4, (dc2tog) 3 times, dc 5 (18 sts).
Round 13: Sl st 6, dc 12 (18 sts).
Round 14: FLO sl st 6, dc 12 in both loops (18 sts).
Round 15: FLO dc 6, dc 12 in both loops (18 sts).
Rounds 16-17: Dc in each st around (18 sts).
Round 18: FLO dc 6 only, (dc2tog) 6 times (12 sts).
Only add stuffing up until round 13, leaving the rest of the leg unstuffed.
Pinch the leg closed, dc through both sides with 6 dc and close the opening (6 sts).
Fasten off and leave a long tail for attaching.

WATER KELPIE

EARS

Make two ears using Blue Whisper colour yarn, working all the stitches in a round from top to bottom. Do not stuff.

Round 1: Make a MC with 4 dc (4 sts).
Round 2: (Dc, dc2inc) twice (6 sts).
Round 3: (Dc2inc) 6 times (12 sts).
Round 4: (Dc, dc2inc) 6 times (18 sts).
Rounds 5-8: Dc in each st around (18 sts).
Do not close the ears. Fasten off and leave a long tail for attaching.

SMALL FINS

Make two fins in Tropical Green colour yarn, working all the stitches in a flat row.

After each row, turn and work back the other way, placing the first dc in the 2nd st from the hook.

Row 1: Ch 9, turn (9 sts).
Row 2: Dc in each ch along, ch, turn (8 sts).
Row 3: Dc in the 3rd loop in each st along, ch 3, turn (8 sts).

The next rows will create the 4 points of the fins.

Row 4: Dc in the 2nd ch from the hook, dc in the next ch, htr in the same stitch as the starting ch, dc, (htr, ch 3, dc in the 2nd ch from hook, dc in the next ch, htr in the same stitch, dc) 3 times (28 sts) (4 points).

Fasten off and leave a long tail for attaching.

BACK FIN

Make a long back fin in Tropical Green colour yarn. Work all stitches in a row.

Row 1: Ch 40, turn (40 sts).
Row 2: Dc 2, (htr, ch 3, dc in the 3rd ch from hook, htr in the same st, dc 2) 11 times, htr, ch 3, dc in the 3rd ch from hook, htr in the same st, dc 3, sl st (68 sts) (12 points).

Fasten off and leave a long tail for attaching.

TAIL FINS

Make two fins in Tropical Green colour yarn, working all the stitches in a flat row.

After each row, turn and work back the other way, placing the first dc in the 2nd st from the hook.

Row 1: Ch 14, turn (14 sts).
Row 2: Dc in each ch across, ch, turn (13 sts).
Row 3: FLO dc 12, (dc 3) in the last st, ch, turn (15 sts).
Row 4: FLO dc in each st across, ch, turn (15 sts).
Row 5: FLO dc 14, (dc 3) in the last st, ch, turn (17 sts).
Row 6: FLO dc in each st across, ch, turn (17 sts).
Row 7: FLO dc 16, (dc 3) in the last st, ch, turn (19 sts).
Row 8: FLO dc in each st across, ch, turn (19 sts).
Row 9: FLO dc 18, (dc 3) in the last st, ch, turn (21 sts).
Row 10: FLO dc in each st across, ch, turn (21 sts).
Row 11: FLO dc 20, (dc 3) in the last st, ch, turn (23 sts).
Row 12: FLO dc in each st across (23 sts).

Fasten off and leave a long tail for attaching.

Weave an embroidery needle with the long yarn tail in and out of the bottom of the fin every 3–4 rows, to make three pleats. Pull tightly to scrunch the pleats on both fins and tie off. Then, with one of the yarn ends, whip stitch the bottom centre three stitches together to connect the two fins. Weave the needle through the back of the whip stitches to fasten off. Last, leave the long yarn tails for attaching the finished fin to the end of the tail.

WATER KELPIE

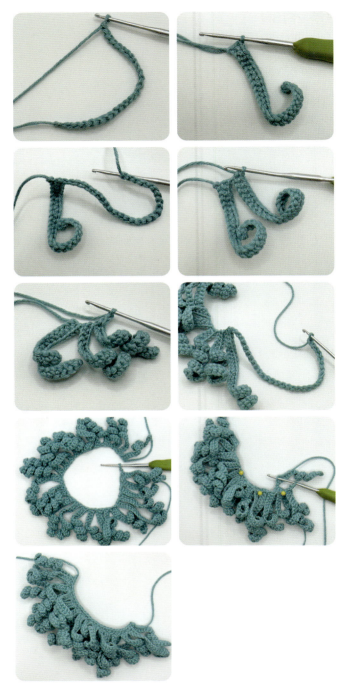

HAIR

Using Turquoise colour yarn, work all the stitches in a flat row.

After each row, turn and work back the other way, placing the first dc in the 2nd st from the hook.

Row 1: Ch 26, turn, dc in each st across (25 sts) (1 hair strand row).

Rows 2-3: Ch 26, turn, dc in each st across (25 sts) (2 rows of hair strands).

Rows 4-25: Ch 31, turn, dc in each st across (30 sts) (22 rows of hair strands).

Rows 26-28: Ch 26, turn, dc in each st across (25 sts) (3 rows of hair strands).

Twist each of the rows to create curls. Fold the hair in half between rows 14 and 15 to pair up a portion of the curls and add a few pins to hold the hair folded in place.

Dc through both sides to create a top seam. There should be approximately 28 dc stitches along the top of the curls to create the seam (28 sts).

Fasten off and leave a long tail for attaching.

STARFISH

Make three starfish in Sunny colour yarn.
Work all the stitches in a round.
Round 1: Make a MC with 10 dc (10 sts).
Round 2: (Htr, ch 3, dc in the 3rd ch from hook, htr in the same st, sl st) 5 times (35 sts) (5 points).
Fasten off, tie both yarn ends together and leave a long tail for attaching.

ATTACHING PIECES AND ASSEMBLY

EYES AND CHEEKS

Details on how to outline the safety eyes in crochet thread can be found in the Finishing Touches section (see page 22).

Using Bubblegum colour yarn, whip stitch or embroider a double line beginning on the round below the safety eyes, starting at the middle of the safety eye and 3 stitches wide. Enter your thread through the bottom of the head and embroider the cheeks. Once finished, bring the needle back down through the head to where it entered. Knot the thread ends together and hide them within the head.

WATER KELPIE

NOSTRILS

Before whip stitching, follow the next steps to place pins marking both nostrils and ensuring they are even with the safety eyes. Mark the nostrils 6 rounds down from the safety eyes, 2 stitches long and 4–5 stitches apart. Then, using a trimmed piece of Blue Whisper yarn about 8in (20cm) long, make two horizontal whip stitches where you marked the nostrils with the pins. Once complete, wrap the embroidery needle and yarn around the horizontal nostril stitches until fully wrapped. When finished, secure and weave in the end.

EARS

Pinch the ears closed and pin them to the top of the head 5–6 rounds above the safety eyes, spaced evenly apart with 8 stitches between them. Angle both ears inward, with the opening to the curved ear facing forward. Once the placement is correct, whip stitch them onto the head using an embroidery needle by putting the needle underneath 2 stitches for the inside and outside of the side of the ear you are working on. Work around the entire ear while keeping the curved shape it was pinned in. When finished, weave in the ends.

CROCHETED MYTHICAL CREATURES

FINS

SMALL FINS
Pin the flat base of the small fins against the lower part of the jaw with the front of the fin facing the safety eyes. One end of the fin should be pinned about 3 stitches below the back of the ear and the other end about 8 stitches straight down from the beginning of the cheek. Attach the flat base with an embroidery needle and the yarn tails, making sure to whip stitch around the ridge made from row 3 in the pattern. Weave in and hide the leftover tail inside the head.

BACK FIN
The long back fin will be pinned on the centre of the back up against the curve of the back and working down to the end of the tail. Use multiple pins to ensure the piece is in the centre of the back before sewing. Whip stitch on with an embroidery needle and the extra yarn tails and weave in the extra yarn end after the fin is sewn in place.

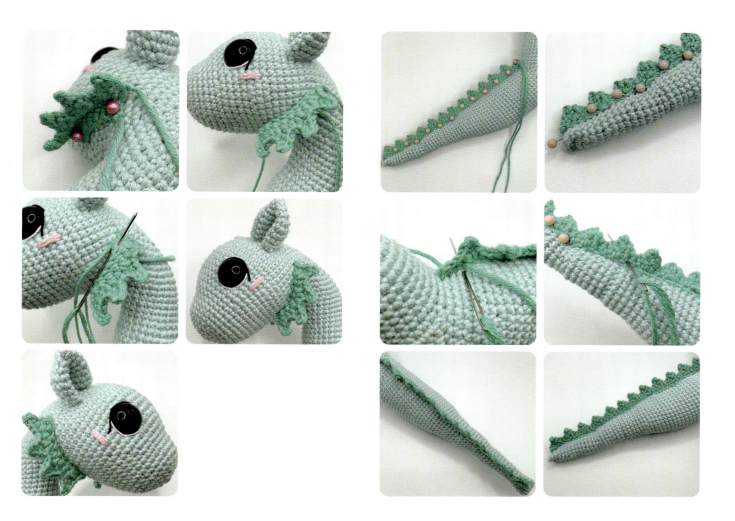

WATER KELPIE

The tail fin should be pinned in three spots before sewing, at the centre and the two sides, to line up the sides of the tail fin and the seam of 6 dc stitches from closing the body. Since all of the leftover yarn ends are in the centre of the tail fin, use an embroidery needle to weave a yarn end through the lower back of the tail fin to get the needle to the side. Then whip stitch the large tail fin to the seam of the tail. Use multiple whip stitches if necessary to attach the tail fin firmly. When secure, weave in all the extra yarn ends into the body.

HAIR

Pin the hair between rounds 13 and 14 on top of the head and centred between the ears, starting with the six shorter curls. Continue pinning the hair piece down the back of the head and neck until it reaches 5–6 rounds above the start of the back fin on the body. Whip stitch the hair to the head and neck with an embroidery needle and the leftover yarn tail. When finished, weave the yarn ends into the head and body.

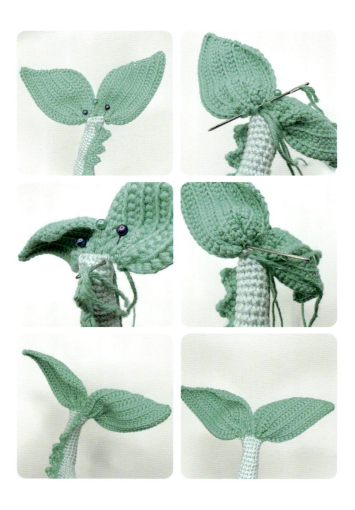

174   CROCHETED MYTHICAL CREATURES

LEGS

Pin the top seam of the legs to the sides of the body between rounds 27 and 28 and 6 stitches between them. With the legs pinned, the knees should be facing outward and the hooves parallel with the surface the kelpie is on. Once the kelpie is standing upright, start whip stitching the seam of the legs in place with an embroidery needle.

If it is not standing upright, adjust the legs up or down to ensure a good standing position before sewing. Add 2–3 whip stitches to the back and front of the legs near the top seam to secure the legs against the body. When the legs are in place and stable, weave in the ends.

STARFISH

The starfish can be sewn on the hair strands at any point in the hair. The exact placement is up to you, but they should be evenly separated with two starfish on the right and one on the left side of the hair. Use an embroidery needle and the leftover yarn tails to whip stitch each of the starfish to the hair. Once finished, tie the two yarn ends from the starfish tightly together, then weave each end into the back of the starfish. Trim off any extra yarn to complete.

WATER KELPIE

MANTICORE

This man-eating hybrid creature is depicted with the body of a lion and the tail of a scorpion. It is thought to have originated within Indian and Persian cultures. The manticore would hunt for villagers in its desolate habitat, killing them with its sharp claws or poisonous tail darts.

Skill Level

Finished size

7in (18cm)

Supplies and materials

Universal Yarn Brand Bamboo Pop DK, 50% cotton, 50% bamboo (292yd/266m per 3½oz/100g): Penny 150, Almond 148, Graphite 120, Chocolate 152, Black 112, True Red 136

Crochet thread 10:
Black and white

Hook size: 2mm

Safety eyes: 9/16in (14mm)

Polyester fibre filling

Embroidery needles

Scissors

Stitch markers

Sewing pins

Pipe cleaners

Stuffing tool or chopstick

HEAD

Using Penny colour yarn, work all stitches in a round from back to front.
Stuff as you crochet.
Round 1: Make a MC with 6 dc (6 sts).
Round 2: (Dc2inc) 6 times (12 sts).
Round 3: (Dc, dc2inc) 6 times (18 sts).
Round 4: (Dc, dc2inc, dc) 6 times (24 sts).
Round 5: (Dc 3, dc2inc) 6 times (30 sts).
Round 6: (Dc 2, dc2inc, dc 2) 6 times (36 sts).
Round 7: (Dc 5, dc2inc) 6 times (42 sts).
Round 8: Dc in each st around (42 sts).
Round 9: (Dc 3, dc2inc, dc 3) 6 times (48 sts).
Round 10: Dc in each st around (48 sts).
Round 11: (Dc 7, dc2inc) 6 times (54 sts).
Rounds 12–15: Dc in each st around (54 sts).
Round 16: (Dc 7, dc2tog) 6 times (48 sts).
Rounds 17–18: Dc in each st around (48 sts).
Round 19: Dc 17, ch, sk, dc 12, ch, sk, dc 17 (48 sts).
Please note: The chain spaces with the skip in round 19 will be where you place the safety eyes later in the pattern.
Round 20: Dc in each st around (48 sts).
Round 21: Dc 9, dc2tog, dc 8, (dc2tog, dc) twice, dc2tog, dc 8, dc2tog, dc 9, dc2tog (42 sts).
Round 22: Dc in each st around (42 sts).
At this time, add the safety eyes in the chain spaces on round 19.
Round 23: (Dc 5, dc2tog) 6 times (36 sts).
Not everyone's tension is the same. When decreasing and increasing in the next 2 rounds, if the stitches are not centred with the safety eyes, adjust the stitches by adding or subtracting 1–2 stitches.
Round 24: Dc 15, (dc2tog) 3 times, dc 15 (33 sts).
Round 25: Dc 16, (dc2inc) 3 times, dc 14 (36 sts).
Round 26: (Dc 2, dc2tog, dc 2) 6 times (30 sts).

Rounds 27–29: Dc in each st around (30 sts).
At this point, if you haven't started to stuff the head, start the stuffing now.
Round 30: (Dc 3, dc2tog) 6 times (24 sts).
Round 31: (Dc, dc2tog, dc) 6 times (18 sts).
Round 32: (Dc, dc2tog) 6 times (12 sts).
Before the last round and fastening off, add more stuffing to the snout and pack it fairly tight to help keep the shape of the head.
Round 33: (Dc, dc2tog) 4 times (8 sts).
Fasten off and weave the yarn under each of the FLO, then pull tight. Bring an embroidery needle down through the centre of the magic circle and out the bottom of the head. Pull slightly to flatten round 33 and hide the end inside the head.

NOSE PANEL

With Penny colour yarn, work in flat rows.
After each row, turn and work back the other way, placing the first dc in the second st from the hook.
Row 1: Ch 7, turn (7 sts).
Rows 2–12: Dc 6, ch, turn (6 sts).
Fasten off and leave a long tail for attaching.

BODY

Using Penny colour yarn, work all stitches in a round from bottom to top.
Stuff as you crochet.
Round 1: Make a MC with 6 dc (6 sts).
Round 2: (Dc2inc) 6 times (12 sts).
Round 3: (Dc, dc2inc) 6 times (18 sts).
Round 4: (Dc, dc2inc, dc) 6 times (24 sts).
Round 5: (Dc 3, dc2inc) 6 times (30 sts).

Round 6: (Dc 2, dc2inc, dc 2) 6 times (36 sts).
Round 7: (Dc 5, dc2inc) 6 times (42 sts).
Round 8: Dc in each st around (42 sts).
Round 9: (Dc 3, dc2inc, dc 3) 6 times (48 sts).
Round 10: Dc in each st around (48 sts).
Round 11: (Dc 7, dc2inc) 6 times (54 sts).
Rounds 12-24: Dc in each st around (54 sts).
Round 25: (Dc 7, dc2tog) 6 times (48 sts).
Rounds 26-29: Dc in each st around (48 sts).
Round 30: (Dc 3, dc2tog, dc 3) 6 times (42 sts).
Rounds 31-32: Dc in each st around (42 sts).
Round 33: (Dc 5, dc2tog) 6 times (36 sts).
Round 34: Dc in each st around (36 sts).
Round 35: (Dc 2, dc2tog, dc 2) 6 times (30 sts).
Round 36: (Dc 3, dc2tog) 6 times (24 sts).
Round 37: Dc 10, htr 10, dc 4 (24 sts).
Fasten off and leave a long tail for attaching.

Rounds 6-9: Dc in each st around (24 sts).
Round 10: (Dc, dc2tog, dc) 6 times (18 sts).
Round 11: Dc 7, (dc2tog) 3 times, dc 5 (15 sts).
Round 12: Dc 7, (dc2inc) 3 times, dc 4, dc2inc (19 sts).
Round 13: Dc2inc, dc 7, dc2inc, dc 3, dc2inc, dc 6 (22 sts).
Round 14: Dc 11, (dc2inc) twice, dc 9 (24 sts).
Round 15: (Dc 3, dc2inc) 6 times (30 sts).
Round 16: (Dc 2, dc2inc, dc 2) 6 times (36 sts).
Round 17: (Dc 5, dc2inc) 6 times (42 sts).
Rounds 18-19: Dc in each st around (42 sts).
Round 20: (Dc 5, dc2tog) 6 times (36 sts).
Round 21: (Dc 2, dc2tog, dc 2) 6 times (30 sts).
Round 22: Dc in each st around (30 sts).
Round 23: (Dc 3, dc2tog) 6 times (24 sts).
Round 24: Dc in each st around (24 sts).
Round 25: (Dc, dc2tog, dc) 6 times (18 sts).
Round 26: (Dc, dc2tog) 6 times (12 sts).
Round 27: (Dc, dc2tog) 4 times (8 sts).
Fasten off and weave the yarn under each of the FLO, pull tight and leave a long tail for attaching.

BACK LEGS

Make two legs in Penny colour yarn.
Work all stitches in a round from bottom to top.
Stuff as you crochet, but do not overstuff. The top portion of the leg on one side needs to be pushed flat when sewn to the body.
Round 1: Make a MC with 6 dc (6 sts).
Round 2: (Dc2inc) 6 times (12 sts).
Round 3: (Dc, dc2inc) 6 times (18 sts).
Round 4: (Dc, dc2inc, dc) 6 times (24 sts).
Round 5: Dc 9, (PUFF, dc) 3 times, PUFF, dc 8 (24 sts).

MANTICORE

ARMS

Make two arms in Penny colour yarn.
Work all stitches in a round from bottom to top.
Stuff as you crochet, but only until round 25, leaving the last few rounds without stuffing.

Round 1: Make a MC with 6 dc (6 sts).
Round 2: (Dc2inc) 6 times (12 sts).
Round 3: (Dc, dc2inc) 6 times (18 sts).
Round 4: (Dc, dc2inc, dc) 6 times (24 sts).
Round 5: Dc 9, (PUFF, dc) 3 times, PUFF, dc 8 (24 sts).
Rounds 6–9: Dc in each st around (24 sts).
Round 10: Dc 9, (dc2tog, dc) twice, dc2tog, dc 7 (21 sts).
Round 11: Dc2tog, dc 19 (20 sts).
Rounds 12–29: Dc in each st around (20 sts).

Pinch the arms closed. If your seam is not parallel with the puff stitches on the foot, add or subtract 1–2 stitches.
Dc through both sides with 10 dc and close the opening (10 sts).
Fasten off and leave a long tail for attaching.

. . . .

EARS

INNER EAR

Make two inner ear pieces in Almond colour.
Work all the stitches in a row.
After turning, place the 1st dc2inc in the 2nd st from the hook.

Round 1: Make a MC with 6 dc, ch, turn (6 sts).
Row 2: (Dc2inc) 6 times (12 sts).
Fasten off the yarn tail. Hiding the leftover yarn will come later in the pattern.

OUTER EAR

Make two outer ear pieces in Penny colour.
Work all the stitches in a row.

Round 1: Make a MC with 6 dc, ch, turn (6 sts).
Row 2: (Dc2inc) 6 times, ch, turn (12 sts).
Row 3: Dc in each st along, ch, turn (12 sts).

Place both the inside and outside parts of the ear together. Make sure both the wrong sides of each piece are facing each other. Dc the next row through both pieces of the ear, making them into one complete ear.

Row 4: (Dc, dc2inc) 6 times (18 sts).

Hide the extra yarn tails inside the bottom opening of the ear. Pinch the ear closed and dc 5 stitches across, closing the opening of the ear and creating a small seam.
Fasten off and leave a long tail for attaching.

HORNS

Make two horns in Graphite colour yarn, working in rounds.
Stuff as you crochet.
Round 1: Make a MC with 4 dc (4 sts).
Round 2: (Dc, dc2inc) twice (6 sts).
Round 3: (Dc, dc2inc, dc) twice (8 sts).
Round 4: (Dc 3, dc2inc) twice (10 sts).
Round 5: (Dc 2, dc2inc, dc 2) twice (12 sts).
Round 6: (Dc2inc) 3 times, dc 3, (dc2tog) twice, dc 2 (13 sts).
Rounds 7–10: Dc in each st around (13 sts).
Round 11: Dc 3, (dc2tog) twice, dc 4, (dc2inc) twice (13 sts).
Round 12: Dc 3, dc2tog, dc 5, dc2inc, dc 2 (13 sts).
Rounds 13–14: Dc in each st around (13 sts).
Fasten off and leave a long tail for attaching.

WINGS

With Black colour yarn, work two wings in flat rows. After each row, turn and work back the other way, placing the first dc in the second st from the hook.
Row 1: Ch 25, turn (25 sts).
Row 2: Dc 24, ch, turn (24 sts).
Row 3: (Htr 3, htr2inc) 6 times, ch, turn (30 sts).
Row 4: Htr in each st along, ch 2, turn (30 sts).
Row 5: FLO tr 2, (tr, ch 3, dc in the 3rd ch from hook, tr in the same st, tr 2) 9 times, tr (48 sts).

Next, fold the wing in half, matching up the tr points, and dc 5 stitches down the first side of the wing and go through both pieces. Then crochet approximately 12 dc stitches along the curved part and go through both pieces. Fasten off and hide the tail inside the wing.

To close the pointed edge of the wing, flip the wing over with the tr points facing upwards. With a long starting tail, attach the Black colour yarn to the 1st stitch on the top right side of the wing. Work approximately 38 dc stitches around the pointed edge to close the wing.
Fasten off and weave the yarn tail into the wing.

MANTICORE

TAIL

Make the tail in True Red colour yarn, working in rounds. Stuff as you crochet.

Round 1: Make a MC with 4 dc (4 sts).
Round 2: (Dc, dc2inc) twice (6 sts).
Round 3: Dc 4, (dc2inc) twice (8 sts).
Round 4: Dc in each st around (8 sts).
Round 5: (Dc, dc2inc) 4 times (12 sts).
Round 6: (Dc, dc2inc) 6 times (18 sts).
Round 7: (Dc2inc) 3 times, dc 4, (dc2tog) 3 times, dc 5 (18 sts).
Round 8: (Dc, dc2inc, dc) 6 times (24 sts).
Rounds 9-10: Dc in each st around (24 sts).
Round 11: (Dc, dc2tog, dc) 6 times (18 sts).
Round 12: Dc in each st around (18 sts).
Round 13: (Dc, dc2tog) 6 times (12 sts).
Round 14: (Dc2tog) 6 times (6 sts).
Round 15: FLO (dc2inc) 6 times (12 sts).
Round 16: (Dc, dc2inc) 6 times (18 sts).
Rounds 17-20: Dc in each st around (18 sts).
Round 21: (Dc, dc2tog) 6 times (12 sts).

Before working round 22, take two pipe cleaners and pair them together. Next, fold them in half and twist the pieces together to make one thick pipe cleaner measuring about 6in (15cm). Insert the twisted pipe cleaners into the tail until it reaches the small opening at round 14. With a stuffing tool, pack in extra stuffing around the pipe cleaner to fill in the second portion of the tail. Then continue to round 22 and crochet around the pipe cleaner.

Round 22: (Dc2tog) 6 times (6 sts).
Round 23: FLO (Dc2inc) 6 times (12 sts).
Round 24: (Dc, dc2inc) 6 times (18 sts).
Rounds 25-27: Dc in each st around (18 sts).
Round 28: (Dc, dc2tog) 6 times (12 sts).

With a stuffing tool, pack in extra stuffing around the pipe cleaner to fill in the third portion of the tail.

Round 29: (Dc2tog) 6 times (6 sts).
Round 30: FLO (Dc2inc) 6 times (12 sts).
Round 31: (Dc, dc2inc) 6 times (18 sts).
Rounds 32-34: Dc in each st around (18 sts).
Round 35: (Dc, dc2tog) 6 times (12 sts).

With a stuffing tool, pack in extra stuffing around the pipe cleaner to fill in the fourth portion of the tail.

Round 36: (Dc2tog) 6 times (6 sts).
Round 37: FLO (Dc2inc) 6 times (12 sts).
Round 38: (Dc, dc2inc) 6 times (18 sts).
Rounds 39-41: Dc in each st around (18 sts).
Round 42: (Dc, dc2tog) 6 times (12 sts).

With a stuffing tool, pack in extra stuffing around the pipe cleaner to fill in the fifth portion of the tail.

Round 43: (Dc2tog) 6 times (6 sts).
Round 44: FLO (Dc2inc) 6 times (12 sts).

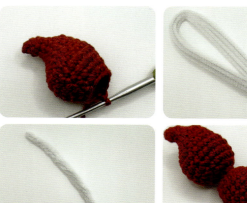

Round 45: (Dc, dc2inc) 6 times (18 sts).
Rounds 46-49: Dc in each st around (18 sts).
Twist the remaining portion of the pipe cleaner in a small circle and push it into the bottom of the last section of the tail.
Round 50: (Dc, dc2tog) 6 times (12 sts).
Add more stuffing to fill the remaining empty space in the bottom of the tail.
Fasten off and leave a long tail for attaching.

MANE
HAIR CAP
Using Chocolate colour yarn, work the hair cap in rounds.
Round 1: Make a MC with 6 dc (6 sts).
Round 2: (Dc2inc) 6 times (12 sts).
Round 3: BLO (Dc, dc2inc) 6 times (18 sts).
Round 4: (Dc, dc2inc, dc) 6 times (24 sts).
Round 5: (Dc 3, dc2inc) 6 times (30 sts).
Round 6: BLO (Dc 2, dc2inc, dc 2) 6 times (36 sts).
Round 7: (Dc 5, dc2inc) 6 times (42 sts).
Round 8: (Dc 3, dc2inc, dc 3) 6 times (48 sts).
Round 9: BLO (Dc 7, dc2inc) 6 times (54 sts).
Rounds 10-11: Dc in each st around (54 sts).
Round 12: BLO dc in each st around (54 sts).
Rounds 13-14: Dc in each st around (54 sts).
Fasten off and leave a long tail for attaching.

HAIR STRANDS
Work the next rounds in chains to create the hair strands. The hair strands are worked in a spiral along the FLO of rounds 3, 6, 9, 12 and 14. When crocheting in a chain, after turning, work the 1st dc stitch in the 2nd chain from the hook. Work from the top to the bottom on the hair cap.
Attach the Chocolate colour yarn to the 1st FLO stitch on round 2. Then, after making round 1 of the six hair strands, continue to work the next chains along the FLO of all the rounds on the hair cap. Do not cut the yarn. The hair curls will spiral around the hair cap in one continuous motion. If they do not curl, gently twist them to the right.
Round 1: Ch 15, turn, dc up the ch, sl st in the next st on the round (repeat to make 12 rows of hair strands).

Beginning with round 2 each hair strand row will end with a sl st in the next 2 FLO to thin out the curls and make the hair cap lighter in weight.
Round 2: Ch 15, turn, dc up the ch, sl st 2 (14 sts) (repeat to make 15 rows of hair strands).
Round 3: Ch 15, turn, dc up the ch, sl st 2 (14 sts) (repeat to make 24 rows of hair strands).
Round 4: Ch 15, turn, dc up the ch, sl st 2 (14 sts) (repeat to make 27 rows of hair strands).
Work the next round on the FLO of round 14 of the hair cap.
Round 5: Ch 15, turn, dc up the ch, sl st 2 (14 sts) (repeat to make only 14 rows of hair strands).
Leave the last FLO stitches on round 14 of the hair cap unworked.
Fasten off and leave a long tail for attaching.

MANTICORE

LOWER MANE

Using Chocolate colour yarn, work in flat rows.
After each row, turn and work back the other way, placing the first dc in the second st from the hook.

Row 1: Ch 25, turn (25 sts).
Row 2: Dc 24, ch, turn (24 sts).
Row 3: FLO dc 24, ch, turn (24 sts).
Row 4: Dc 24, ch, turn (24 sts).
Row 5: FLO dc 24, ch, turn (24 sts).

Fasten off and weave in the extra yarn end. Attach the Chocolate colour yarn to the first BLO st on row 2 with a sl st. Work the next rows in chains to create the hair strands. When crocheting in a chain, after turning, work the first dc stitch in the second chain from the hook. Then sl st to the next stitch before starting the next hair strand row.

Hair strand rows 1–24: Ch 25, turn, dc 24 up the ch, sl st (24 sts) (24 rows of hair strands).

After hair strand 24, sl st to the BLO of row 4 to continue to work the next set of chains.

Hair strand rows 25–49: Ch 25, turn, dc 24 up the ch, sl st (24 sts) (24 rows of hair strands).

After hair strand 48, sl st to the 1st BLO of row 2.
Fasten off and leave a long tail for sewing.
If the hair strands do not curl on their own, gently twist them to the right.

ATTACHING PIECES AND ASSEMBLY

EYES

Details on how to outline the safety eyes in crochet thread can be found in the Finishing Touches section (see page 22).

NOSE PANEL AND DETAILS

Using pins, secure the nose piece to the front of the face between the safety eyes at rounds 17–18 and ending at rounds 30–31. Leave about 2 stitches between each safety eye and the sides of the nose panel. With an embroidery needle and the leftover yarn tail, whip stitch the panel in place. Enter the needle through the nose at the corner of the panel, up through the first stitch, and back down through the face. Then continue whip stitching around the nose panel until it is attached to the face. Once finished, weave in the yarn end and hide it within the head.

To create a small triangle nose, mark the nose with 3 pins; first, at each corner between rows 11 and 12 of the panel and another 3 rounds down the face and centre. Using black crochet thread and an embroidery needle, enter the needle through the bottom of the head and then out at the bottom pin. Embroider a line to each pin, ensuring the nose keeps its shape. From there, whip stitch (see page 21) the triangle in a fan-like shape, working from one side to the other, filling in the spaces between each threaded line. Once finished, outline the top of the nose with a few whip stitches. Bring the needle down through the head, tie the thread ends together and hide them within the head.

MANTICORE

LEGS AND ARMS

Tilt the body forward with the htr from the last round on the top, and pin the flat portion of the legs to the sides of the body starting between rounds 25 and 26. At the widest part of the legs, leave 16 stitches between them on the front and back of the body. With the legs pinned, the feet should be down and parallel to the surface. If the body is sitting, whip stitch using an embroidery needle around the large thigh part of the legs only. If the body is not sitting, take this time to adjust the legs up or down to ensure a good sitting position.

Add 1–2 extra whip stitches to the inside of the foot and round 9 of the body to keep the legs secure. When finished, weave in the ends.

Pin the arms against the legs in the space between the top of the legs and the open neck portion of the body. Please note that the seam of the arms will be at an angle and not aligned with the rows because of the tilted position of the body. Leaving 1–2 stitches between the top of the arms and the last round of the body, add an extra pin to the inside of the leg near the feet to keep them in place for sewing. If they are even, touching the surface and the body is still sitting, whip stitch the arms to the body using an embroidery needle. If not, take this time to adjust the arms up or down to ensure a good placement.

Add 2–3 whip stitches to the back of the arms near the top seam to secure the legs against the body. Do this also at the inside of the foot and round 12 of the body, keeping the arms secure. When the arms are in place and stable, weave in the ends.

HEAD AND BODY

Before attaching the head to the body, use pins to ensure the placement is correct. You want the back of the neck to match up between rounds 10 and 11 of the back of the head and centred. Make sure that the nose is centred between the arms. Once aligned and centred, whip stitch the pieces together in a circle using an embroidery needle and the long tail left over from the body. When finished, weave in the end.

ATTACHING THE MANE

Match up the MC of the mane and the MC of the head and add a pin to the top of the hair to keep it in place. The last round of 14 hair strands should be in the front of the face evenly spaced above the eyes on round 12 of the head. Whip stitch the rim of the mane between rounds 12 and 13 of the head using an embroidery needle and the long yarn tail.

MANTICORE

LOWER MANE

Wrap the lower mane under the chin and pin the ends to the rim of the hair cap next to the first and the last hair strands. This is the last round of hair strands above the safety eyes. Using an embroidery needle and the leftover yarn tail, whip stitch 4 stitches to attach the end of the lower mane to the bottom of the hair cap. Do not cut the yarn, but weave the needle through the hair cap and out the other side near the other pin. Whip stitch 4 stitches to attach the other side of the lower mane to the hair cap. When secure, weave in the yarn end and hide it in the mane.

EARS

Pin the ears to the top of the head between the two layers of hair strands directly above the safety eyes. Both ears should be spaced evenly with 8–9 stitches between them. Once the placement is correct, whip stitch to the head with an embroidery needle and the leftover yarn tail from each ear. When finished, weave in the ends.

HORNS

Pin the horns above the ears, behind the next round of hair strands with 8–9 stitches spaced between each of them. The points of the horns should be facing towards each other. When centred, use an embroidery needle and whip stitch around the horns to attach the pieces securely. Once complete, weave in and hide the leftover tails inside the head.

WINGS

Pin the wings to the body in the centre of the back. Flip the wings where the 5 treble points are on the bottom, and the fastened-off stitches from both wings are touching in the centre of the back. Space the tops of the wing with 7 stitches between them. Then, using an embroidery needle and the long leftover yarn ends from the wings, whip stitch the 6 stitches above the fastened-off stitches of each wing to the back of the manticore. When you have finished sewing, weave the ends into the body.

TAIL

The tail should be pinned to get the correct placement before sewing. It should be attached on the lower back about 8–9 rounds below the wings, centred and angled to the upper right above the right wing. Once in place, sew the tail using an embroidery needle and the leftover yarn tail to whip stitch it onto the back. Then weave the end into the body to hide it.

MANTICORE

ABOUT THE AUTHOR

Jacki Donhou is a native of Las Vegas, Nevada, who learned to crochet after moving to Washington State and becoming a stay-at-home mum. After a few years of following other people's designs, she decided to try creating her own, inspired by her love of animals and her memories of her kids and how they loved their favourite toys when they were growing up. Since then, she has developed a loyal social media following as people have fallen in love with her unique and fun amigurumi designs.

Now living on the East Coast, fuelled by coffee, giggles and a strange addiction to colourful yarn, Jacki is always looking for new ways to make people smile.

Jacki's first book, *Yarn Cake Amigurumi,* was also published by GMC Publications. This crochet pattern book is filled with cute amigurumi patterns that teach you how to create adorable animals in fun colours using colourful yarn cakes.

INDEX

abbreviations 23

Banshee 92
BLO (back loop only) 17
BOB (bobble stitch) 16

Cerberus 45
ch (chain stitch) 11
changing colours 19
Cherry Blossom Dryad 104
Chinese Dragon 72
crochet hooks 8
crochet thread 8

dc (double crochet) 12
dc2inc 14
dc2tog 14
Djinn 54
dtr (double treble) 13

embroidery needles 9
fasten off 20
Faun 62

FLO (front loop only) 17

Griffin 124
hair: loop and hook 22
holding a hook 10
holding yarn 10
htr (half treble) 13
htr2inc 14
htr2tog 15

Kraken 36

Manticore 176
mattress stitch 21
MC (magic circle) 16
Medusa the Gorgon 26
Mermaid 138

Nessie the Loch Ness Monster 84

pipe cleaners 9
pompoms 9
POP (popcorn stitch) 18

PUFF (puff stitch) 17

safety eyes 9, 22
scissors 9
sewing pins 9
slipknot 11
sl st (slip stitch) 11
stitch markers 9
stuffing 9

tr (treble) 12
tr2inc 14
tr2tog 15

Unicorn 114

Water Kelpie 162
weaving in ends 20
whip stitch 21
Wolpertinger 150

yarn 8
yarn over or under 19